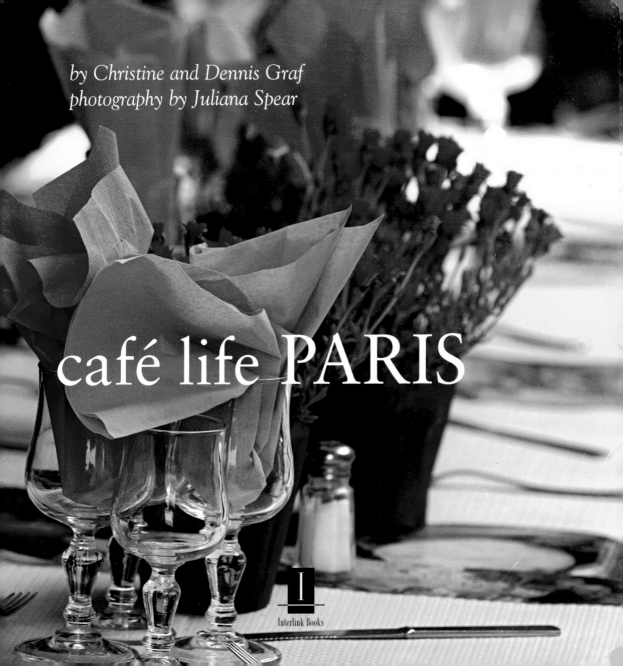

by Christine and Dennis Graf
photography by Juliana Spear

# café life PARIS

Interlink Books

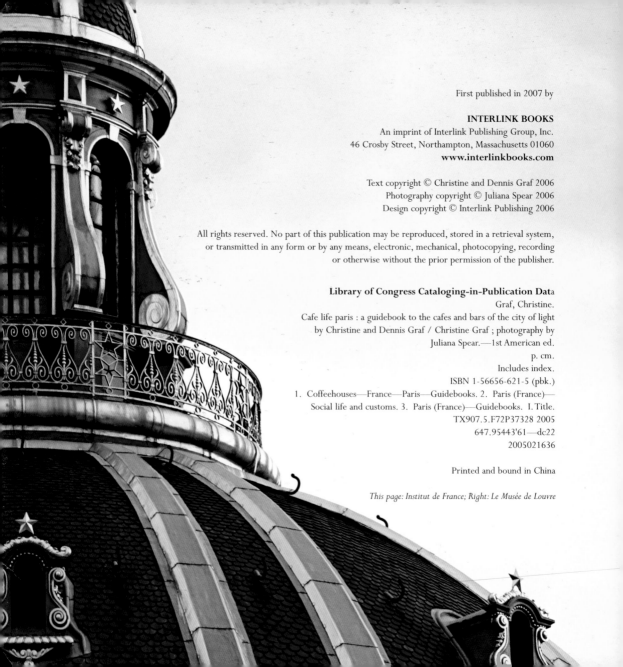

First published in 2007 by

**INTERLINK BOOKS**
An imprint of Interlink Publishing Group, Inc.
46 Crosby Street, Northampton, Massachusetts 01060
**www.interlinkbooks.com**

**Library of Congress Cataloging-in-Publication Data**
Graf, Christine.
Cafe life paris : a guidebook to the cafes and bars of the city of light
by Christine and Dennis Graf / Christine Graf ; photography by
Juliana Spear.—1st American ed.
p. cm.
Includes index.
ISBN 1-56656-621-5 (pbk.)
1. Coffeehouses—France—Paris—Guidebooks. 2. Paris (France)—
Social life and customs. 3. Paris (France)—Guidebooks. I. Title.
TX907.5.F72P37328 2005
647.95443'61—dc22
2005021636

Printed and bound in China

*This page: Institut de France; Right: Le Musée de Louvre*

*To a magical city and the friends we have found there*

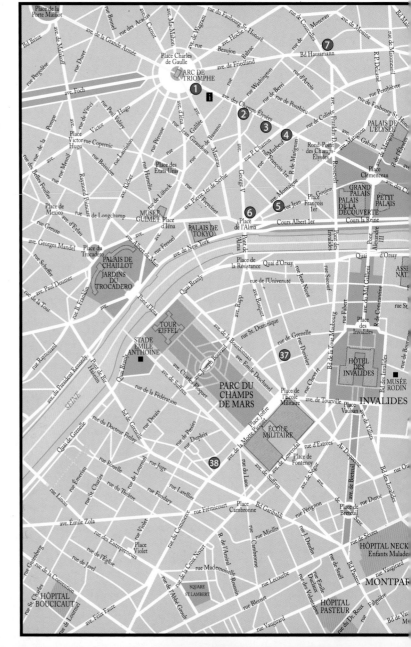

# INTRODUCTION

*You start at a café table because everything in Paris starts at a café table.*
—Irwin Shaw, *Paris! Paris!*

What could be more Parisian than a café? Imagine smoke-filled rooms dotting the city, frequented over the years by Sartre and Simone de Beauvoir, Picasso, James Joyce, Fitzgerald, Hemingway, and later by Richard Wright, James Baldwin, and many others. Picture sophisticated salons with elaborate *boiserie* illuminated in gold—these, too, can be cafés serving drinks in the afternoons. Here in the City of Light is an extraordinary variety of places in which to cultivate the art of living as only the French can. Despite the intrusions of fast food, punitive taxes, and trendy foreign imports, the French café still retains a life of its own and an amazing vitality.

The Parisian café is one of the best-loved symbols of the city, although its image for most people is undefined. Everyone knows what the Eiffel Tower or the Arc de Triomphe looks like, but many in America or Great Britain have had their idea of Parisian cafés formed from the romantic depictions in movies and on television. One thinks of Audrey Tautou tending bar in *Amélie* or of Audrey Hepburn dancing in *Funny Face* inside a cafe that was pure Hollywood.

The first café in Paris was Le Procope, founded in 1702 by a Sicilian, Francesco Procopio dei Coltelli. By 1789 there were many cafés, and leaders of the Revolution frequented them. A few years later, Napoleon was playing chess at the Café Régence. The nineteenth century was the great age of the French café. It was a period when luxurious cafés on the Grands Boulevards were the places for fashionable people to go and be seen. Charles Dickens, in his *Dictionary of Paris: An Unconventional Handbook*, published in 1882, mentioned 20 leading cafés; of that group, only the Café de la Paix exists as a café today, although Le Procope—now an unexceptional restaurant—is also mentioned. He described the role of the café in the city:

> The café is not a club, but it is made to take the place of a club by many hundreds, who go there to see their friends. Birds of a feather, we are told, like to congregate; and in these houses men of the same class, of the same trade or profession, or any small circle of friends, will often meet together by chance or from habit, not very definitely predetermined when... frequenters of cafés are supposed to be in perpetual exuberance of spirits, always witty, always happy, and each one the best fellow in the world.

Although the café has been hailed as the world's most democratic institution, in the nineteenth century the great cafés on the Grands Boulevards were reserved for the upper classes. As Georges Montorgeuil, a commentator at the time, wrote:

> It was an audacious fellow or a boor who dared set foot in the old Café de Paris without a sponsor. Tortoni's had its own set, and no one felt at home in the Grand Balcon until after the proper introductions had been made.

Later, in the 1890s, the café scene was taken up by the middle class and thus lost its interest for the aristocracy. Tortoni's, the Café de Paris, and the Café de Madrid, having lost their clientele, all closed within a few years of each other.

Cafés continued to be separate according to social class. W. Scott Haine has observed in *The World of the Paris Café*, there wasn't much social mixing in nineteenth-century cafés: "the typical working-class café was characterized as a shop with no gas, few chairs, but a lot of smoke." Middle-class people doubted if workers would behave properly in public; they complained that working-class establishments smelled, and objected to the smoking there.

In our time people meet at cafés to read, drink coffee, beer, wine, or soft drinks, to talk, flirt, haggle, relax, study, and, more frequently now, to compose on their laptops. A dog may be patiently waiting alongside. Cafégoers log on to the internet and read the news from their home cities of Boston or Tokyo. Tourists write postcards. We've even seen some people doze off.

The coffee served in most cafés is basic espresso. It's a dark, rather bitter and thick brew that many people find is an acquired taste. Visitors to Paris often prefer to order it *allongé*—diluted with hot water, referred to elsewhere as "café Américain"—and sometimes *deca*—decaffeinated.

There's an arcane system of pricing in most cafés. If you stand at the bar, the price you pay will be a fraction, often half, of what your drink will cost if you sit at a table. If you sit outside on the terrace, the price may be still higher. There's a good reason for the difference: café owners have to pay higher taxes on drinks served at tables and terraces than at the bar.

The old corner café, where little was available but a drink and a simple *demi-baguette* sandwich or *croque-monsieur*—the traditional toasted ham-and-cheese sandwich—has largely disappeared. To survive, many café owners have had to hire a *cuisinier* and offer a lunch *formule*, or menu. It's not unusual to see a small café with a blackboard outside featuring the day's specials. If all you wish is a drink, you may decide to avoid the café at peak hours—12 to 2:00PM for lunch, 7:30 to 10:00PM for dinner—or to look for the few tables that are not obviously set for a meal.

Consider the *cafetiers*, the café owners. They are as varied as the cafés they tend. Some described to us how they experienced strong emotions when they first set eyes on "their" café, a feeling they can only describe as being much like falling in love, and how they bought it despite their doubts and concerns about the risks and responsibilities of this new life.

A proprietress from the Auvergne (a mountainous region in the center of France) who owns two cafés near the Place des Vosges in the Marais pointed out the difficulties of coming to Paris and trying to start a café: "What it takes is courage. The generation of my grandfather—they didn't have much education. But they came here, they started this, and they had courage."

A great many Auvergnats came to Paris in the early part of the twentieth century. The first generation brought coal from the mines in Auvergne to Paris. Their sons started *bougnats*, places where they kept a café and sold coal. (*Bougnat* is a shortened form of the word *charbonnier*, or seller of coal. Both the cafés where coal was sold and their proprietors were often referred to as *bougnats*.)

Some Auvergnats succeeded beyond their wildest dreams. Marcellin Cazes started the Brasserie Lipp. Like many other Auvergnats, Cazes started out working in Paris as a *porteur d'eau*, a water carrier, expected to deliver a copper bathtub and warm water to individual customers upon request, much as icemen used to deliver blocks of ice in the summer to their customers in the United States. In the winters, it is said, Parisians didn't bathe very often, so they needed to buy less hot water. Some water carriers then took up the selling of coal, and sold wine and other drinks as well.

Paul Chambon, "scarcely out of his peasant's smock," according to one observer, started the Dôme in Montparnasse. Other Auvergnats founded the Café de Flore and the Deux Magots. Former *bougnats* include two attractive bistros in the 11th arrondissement, the Bistrot du Peintre and Jacques Mélac. (The city of Paris is divided into districts, called arrondissements, but colloquially these are referred to by number only—as "the 11th," for instance; we shall refer to them this way as well from here on.)

One of the best pictures of an Auvergnat café owner has been left to us by Simone de Beauvoir, remembering Paul Boubal at the Café de Flore during the war years. She recalled:

> I loved the moment when Boubal, a blue apron tied around him, came bustling into the still empty café and began to bring his little world to life again. He lived in a flat over the premises... A pair of bloodshot eyes would blink at one from the tough, solid Auvergne face; for the first hour or so he would remain in a perfectly filthy temper. He would shout out orders, irritably, to the kitchen hand... [H]e would also discuss the previous night's goings-on with the waiters, Jean and Pascal, and send back a stinking cup of ersatz coffee...

The importance of *cafés arabes*—cafés owned, for the most part, by immigrants from Algeria—was pointed out to us by a proprietor of a café near the Cirque d'Hiver (Winter Circus). He told us that Algerians are second only to Auvergnats as the group owning the most Parisian cafés.

The first café owned by an Algerian was opened in 1918 in the rue de Chartres. Arab cafés grew numerous in the working-class sections of Paris, where they played an essential role in the cultural and social life of new immigrants from North Africa. More recently cafés with proprietors whose parents or grandparents came to France from North Africa can be found in the more affluent districts: l'Entrée des Artistes, Le Café Universel, and La Charette are examples of such cafés.

If you wonder whether the French café will still be important in the twenty-first century, take a look at our choices. They are grand and impressive; they are famous and celebrated; they are small and unknown. They dominate a square, or are discreetly hidden on back streets. They cater to business people, to the fashionable set, to tourists, tradespeople, and students. Whatever their specific situation is, they offer you the best vantage point for getting to know Paris and its people. You won't find Parisians lined up in front of the monuments or trying to "do" the Louvre in a day: you will find many of them engaged in animated discussions at the bar or observing street life from the *terrasse* of a café. And if you know a few words of French, or sit next to a young French person eager to try out that school English, you'll start to develop a real understanding of this city.

· 1 ·

# GREAT & GLAMOROUS PLACES

*And now, quite suddenly in the second half of the nineteenth century, the general image of Paris became that of a city with clean wide streets, well lit and well frequented, where everything was done to amuse the visitor. You... had your choice of the best food and wine in the world, you could go to the theater and the opera, and you were yourself part of a continuous street entertainment that was the envy of every other city in the world.*

—John Russell, *Paris*

*C*ome with us to observe Paris from the legendary cafés. They are as significant in the life of the French capital as any monument. These cafés include names that resonate throughout the world: they happen to be in Paris, but their clientele is international. They have received wealthy private individuals and celebrities, and have assumed an importance quite beyond their choice location.

The most opulent, the most expensive, the most famous café in Paris, or probably anywhere in the world, is the Café de la Paix, across from the old Opéra. When you see a painting of a massive and extravagant Parisian building with a glittering sidewalk café to the left, it's invariably this opera house and this café. It's certainly one of the most famous images of Paris, instantly recognizable by people who have never set foot in France.

The Café de la Paix exudes glamour. You might be sitting at the spot on the terrace where Oscar Wilde glimpsed the fluttering of angels' wings. (Skeptics claim that he saw the reflection of the gilded statues atop the Opera.)

Fouquet's, at the intersection of the Champs-Elysées and the avenue George V, is another such place. Top people in film and theater have always gone there. Irwin Shaw in Paris! Paris! recalls a group that would gather in the late evenings at a similar, but no longer existing, bar on that avenue:

> on the Avenue George V, where every midnight your American friends would congregate, as in a club, Bob Capa drawling out his Hungarian-accented English, a cigarette drooping from his mouth… John Huston, in town to make *Moulin Rouge*… Gene Kelly, for *An American in Paris*…. Billy Wilder, caustically witty, in town for the shooting of *Love in the Afternoon*… Art Buchwald, the next day's column just finished, looking for a poker game…

On a cloudy day, such a café is an ideal spot for meeting a friend. It is one of those magic places that make one feel, for a time at least, particularly privileged and secure. You'll understand Audrey Hepburn in the role of Holly Golightly and her need to "breakfast" in front of Tiffany's: "It calms me down right away, the quietness and the proud look of it; nothing very bad can happen to you there…"

# La Coupole

**102 blvd du Montparnasse, 75014**
**(01.43.20.14.20)**
**Métro: Vavin**
**Open daily 8:30AM–1:00AM**

A loud, Deco swirl of activity, seemingly more Manhattan than Montparnasse: Primitive nudes painted in strident colors on the pillars. Crowds of *BCBG—bon chic bon genre*, French yuppies—proper business people, trendsetters out on the town. From them issues a clamor of collective gratification.

And at the bar you see all the blond wood, the courteous servers, the retro green of the pillars that dominate the *grande salle*, all of them topped with the lively, outrageous paintings.

The Jazz Age somehow doesn't seem that far away at the Coupole. For one thing, it's not tarted up like its venerable neighbors, the Dome and the Rotonde, but has been faithfully restored.

The Coupole is a legend. Georges Simenon, who worked on two of his mysteries sitting in this café, made it the setting for much of the action in *Maigret's War of Nerves*,

one of the best in the Maigret series. Fashion setters come here to see and be seen. We hear a babble of voices in many languages—introductions, exchanges of polite formulas. Some people exchange *la bise*, the polite cheek-kissing that we associate with Paris.

On a nighttime bar crawl down the boulevard du Montparnasse, if your doctor or your conscience forbids much ale or wine, try the lighter fare—sip a *deca* (decaffeinated coffee) on the terrace.

There's a flurry of excitement here, a surge of energy such as you sense in the great *brasseries*, loud and boisterous late-night places with a Germanic flavor about them. You see white-haired *intellos*, distinguished-looking gentlemen escorting noticeably younger women, correctly-suited business people leading their clients about on a night on the town. Alive, brash, electric: there's nothing in town quite like La Coupole. The latest in cocktails and champagne specials is chalked up in pastels on the *ardoises* at the bar; a *grand cru* of Pommery champagne is there for a celebration.

You hear the French trying out their English on their foreign equivalents, valiantly struggling with our "th" and other difficult Anglo-Saxon sounds. The foreigners approach the famous bar, asking for a *bière pression* or a *vin blanc* and getting instant service from the energetic barman. Cheerful, sprightly, with a life of its own that defies trends, ignores what's in and out, the Coupole is a great institution with more real *joie de vivre* than most.

# *Fouquet's*

**99 avenue des Champs-Elysées, 75008 (01.47.23.50.00)**
**Métro: George V**
**Open daily 8AM–2AM**

Actress Charlotte Rampling comes to Fouquet's. So, in the old days, did Elizabeth Taylor and Richard Burton, and before them, Marlene Dietrich. This was Orson Welles's favorite hangout on the Champs-Elysées. Earlier, the Duke and Duchess of Windsor would stop by. James Joyce was a regular. And Rita Hayworth fell in love with Aly Khan over a table at Fouquet's. Jean-Paul Belmondo and Gérard Dépardieu number among its contemporary patrons. If you are to spot a famous face in Paris, it will probably be here, and if you take a table by the window, you'll find passersby throwing glances at you, wondering who you are. Your fellow patrons might well include an Italian gentleman clad in a light-colored Brioni silk suit. The next table might host pretty girls doffing their long black coats.

There are few more opulent cafés in Paris. The rich and highly polished brass bar is a thing of splendor probably unmatched in the city. All is gilt and crystal and velvet.

Each of the little black lacquered tables might have a small vase with an orchid looking out at you. The heavy old-fashioned velour-covered armchairs fit one like a Saville Row suit. The inner spaces suggest the first-class public rooms in a great hotel.

At Fouquet's you sit at a small black table, drinking outrageously priced but well-flavored coffee accompanied by miniature muffins. You might get better coffee at a hole-in-the wall *café-tabac* on the rue Mouffetard. But that's not the Champs-Elysées, and the Arc de Triomphe is nowhere in sight.

*Parisiennes* from this area sometimes stop by after shopping, willing to pay five euros for coffee to avoid the crowds on the Champs-Elysées. There's a steady procession of well-fed, well-dressed *bourgeoises*, many in furs to guard against the December chill. A few wealthy-looking tourists stop in. People may think they come here for refuge, but soon they'll be in touch with their acquaintances by cell phone. Even here.

In warm weather people pay Fouquet's prices for the privilege of sitting at tables out on the sidewalk under the red-and-gold awning. We found the interior, however, with waiters gliding noiselessly about, a flower on every table, little lamps casting the most discreet light, and a wealth of red lilies, to be infinitely more appealing.

# *Le Café Marly*

**93 rue de Rivoli, 75001**
**(01.49.26.06.60)**
**Métro: Palais Royal–Musée du Louvre**
**Open daily 8AM–2AM**

*P*aris has, as one might expect, more than its share of designer cafés: chic, elegant, and usually expensive places where the food is secondary, the coffee ordinary, and the clientele young and photogenic. Many of these cafés have been owned by the Costes brothers. Their most famous and talked-about café was the Café Costes, and during its brief and rather spectacular appearance on a dingy street not far from the Pompidou Museum, it attracted international attention for its cutting-edge design. Even the men's washroom was surrealistic, and a man relieving himself against an indescribable backlit wall of frosted glass found it almost an otherworldly experience.

The Café Marly is in this tradition. When it opened a few years ago, it garnered great publicity, and was covered in the *New York Times* and almost everywhere else. From the beginning, elegantly dressed young people of indeterminate nationality and often ambiguous sexuality gathered here. Many of them seemed to know each other. They could have been models and photographers and editors, people from the French fashion world. A sleek and glossy crowd had found a home, and they were not particularly concerned about the high prices and the rather ordinary cuisine. Most of them had the slender silhouettes of people who do not normally pay attention to food. Now it seems as if much of this group has moved on, probably to another fashionable spot.

If you're fortunate enough to arrive on a warm day, you'll want to sit outside in the corridor under the magnificently carved arches. And if your view seems fit for a king, it used to be just that. The Louvre, where the Café Marly is situated, was a royal palace, started during the reign of Francis I and completed during the nineteenth century. You'll gaze over the inner courtyard and view the crowds lining up to enter through the large glass pyramid of I. M. Pei, one of the few avant-garde constructions of which most Parisians approve.

# Café du Musée Jacquemart-André

**158 blvd Haussmann, 75008 (01.45.62.11.59); Métro: Miromesnil. Open daily 11:45AM–5:30PM (museum entry not required).**

A hundred and some years ago you would not have been sipping your coffee in this palatial room, now the café of the Musée Jacquemart-André. It was then the formal dining room of one of the great mansions of the city of Paris, the family home of one of the richest and most important bankers in the city. Here are dark oaken floors polished by decades of servants. Tall windows draped with heavy French fabric open onto a large terrace. You'll see impossibly high ceilings with a large fresco by Tiepolo, brought from a villa near Venice. Oil paintings, velvet chairs, Oriental rugs. Gilt, silver, tapestry. It was all intended to impress and it still does.

In warm weather people walk through this room, look around, and then step outside to the elegant terrace overlooking the well-maintained grounds, adorned with statues and small, formal hedges. This is a perfect spot on a warm day to enjoy the *sorbet*. We suggest the melon, if it's available.

# Café de la Paix

**Place de l'Opéra, 75009**
**(01.40.07.32.32)**
**Métro: Opéra**
**Open daily 10AM–1AM**

Sir Arthur Conan Doyle used to revise the Sherlock Holmes stories while seated at the Café de la Paix. And Victor Hugo held banquets in the *salons*, which have been restored to their original Second Empire style. When he was in Paris, Noel Coward spent hours at the Café de la Paix contemplating the passersby. So did the Duke of Windsor.

"One afternoon I was sitting outside the Cafe de la Paix, watching the splendour and shabbiness of Parisian life, and wondering over my vermouth at the strange panorama of pride and poverty that was passing before me," wrote Oscar Wilde at the beginning of the story "The Sphinx Without A Secret." The amazing thing is that you can see the Café and the great Opéra across from it looking much as they did when Wilde was there.

What you see inside is lavish over-the-top luxury, excesses in the manner of baroque palaces, with gilded pillars and intricate framing of murals and fanciful decoration. And what a ceiling! It includes all manner of shapes: lozenges, squares, circles, and

triangles, surrounded by gold framing and with skies and flowers painted within.

Closer to your table, elaborate little lamps shed a warm light: there's a five-branched lamp, each with its small shade, on the side sconces, and a nine-branched light fixture in the center. The tables are green-veined marble in dark wood, larger than the typical café table, but not the brass-edged white marble that remains the classic in most cafés.

Here is a clientele that exudes self-assurance and is at ease in this extraordinary interior. Their Burberry raincoats are set off by exotic dark designer scarves. Heavy plate glass on the terrace separates them from the people outside, walking quickly past but always glancing in, hoping to see a famous face.

The service is pleasantly unrushed. We notice an older man with a younger woman; groups of middle-aged women, well-preserved and well-coiffed; a mother followed by her son, a young boy with impeccable manners. Heavy-set businessmen from several cultures engage in pleasant banter across the tables.

The look here is special to this café. Instead of the typical red moleskin banquettes, these are done in green velvet, flanked by voluminous curtains of pale ivory that separate the terrace from the dining room. Plain green pillars topped in gold lead to the terrace. Within are more elaborate, gilded pillars, crowned by complicated capitals. Even the waiters' station is unusual. It's not the typical cupboard-like arrangement of old wood with slots for cutlery and napkins. Here it's a sleek piece of furniture in polished wood, the doors enhanced with a metallic sunburst motif.

The Café de la Paix is not intimidating, though. The effect is elegant yet inviting, well-lit, and pleasing. A large floor lamp near each small table makes it easy to read the paper or see your companion. The café side is good on a cool night, when you enjoy the warmth of the lavish interior. We don't recommend sitting outside on the terrace with the hapless tourists who sip their espresso in the fumes of enormous tour and city buses that sweep around the great Place de l'Opéra, but this glassed-in porch is very special.

We like to imagine Oscar Wilde here, reveling in the gilded baroque luxury of this overdone interior, rooms that go well with Garnier's fanciful wedding-cake of an Opéra across the street. Sometimes warmth and luxury and outrageous overuse of gilded scrolls and flower chains seem just about right; they can even have a soothing effect.

People come here to bask in the luxury of it all—to sip a drink, sample an elaborate dessert, meet a friend on the terrace of one of the world's best-known cafés.

· 2 ·

# LEGENDS OF LITERATURE & ART

*One evening after chatting with Ionesco in his apartment on the boulevard Montparnasse I invited him to have coffee in the Falstaff. I had become on good terms with this puckish character... When we went in, Beckett was sitting with Con Leventhal, just inside the door. Observing the usual code, I did not mix guests. Ionesco may have given Beckett a nod, but no more; on the other hand Beckett and Sartre never exchanged a glance.*

*Sartre was already there... But to my astonishment, so was Jean-Luc Godard, who'd never before been in the place, sitting with two friends, paying no attention to anyone. Considering that the Falstaff had only about nine tables, this was probably one of the greatest concentrations of talent per square foot Paris had ever seen outside the cemetery at Père Lachaise.*

—Peter Lennon, *Foreign Correspondent: Paris in the Sixties*

*W*riters have long been drawn to the Left Bank cafés. F. Scott Fitzgerald, already well known for This Side of Paradise, met Ernest Hemingway for the first time at the Dingo Bar, a café that no longer exists; later, during their second meeting at the Closerie des Lilas, he showed him the manuscript of The Great Gatsby. Hemingway composed much of The Sun Also Rises at the Closerie. James Baldwin's argument with Richard Wright at the Deux Magots led to a break in their relationship. Baldwin wrote parts of Go Tell It On the Mountain upstairs at the Flore. And in the Deux Magots plaques mark the favorite tables of many writers, including Jean-Paul Sartre and Simone de Beauvoir.

For many of the young people who went to live in Paris after World War I, the cafés turned into an extension of home. Expatriates found that the discomfort and loneliness of chilly, dimly lit hotel rooms was enough to drive them to the warmth of the cafés. There the quiet, reserved behavior of the French and their respect for other people's privacy allowed creativity to flower. As the great photographer Brassaï mentions in his biography of Henry Miller:

> Of all his new discoveries, Henry was most delighted by those oases of peace and idleness that can be found in all Latin countries, and which abound in Paris: sidewalk cafés. For the simple price of a cup of coffee or a beer, you could write, talk, listen to conversations, meet people, daydream, people-watch, and let the world go by. This was a form of recreation almost unknown to anyone living in America at the time, and what truly amazed Henry was that it all cost so little. We sometimes spent entire days in the cafés.

*Why did so many American and English artists and writers choose to go to Paris in the first place? One would have expected them to prefer English-speaking London, artistic and decadent Berlin, or charming and sunny Rome. Instead, they flocked to Paris—perhaps to get away from Prohibition, possibly hoping to experience the sensual pleasures of a city unaffected by Puritan notions of morality. The stunning Belle Epoque posters of Jules Chéret and Toulouse-Lautrec, among other artists, with scantily-clad women flaunting their sexuality, seemed to promise a* culture free from the Victorian prudery affecting most "Anglo-Saxons," as the French refer to the English and Americans among them. A steep drop in the value of French currency made Paris affordable: at the beginning of 1920 one dollar bought a month's supply of bread. Once people started going to the French capital, the growing English-speaking community there attracted others to the city. Years after his stay in Paris, writer Harold Stearns described the scene in the Montparnasse cafés: "A seething madhouse of drunks, semi-drunks, quarter-drunks and sober maniacs... It was a useless, silly life and I have missed it every day since."

One of the best accounts of an expatriate's experiences in the Left Bank cafés was written by Morley Callaghan in That Summer in Paris:

> For a few blocks Montparnasse was a dismal stretch of boulevard, but then we came to the Raspail corner and the cafés. On one corner was the Dôme, which not long ago had been merely a zinc bar with a small

terrace; now it was like the crowded bleachers at an old ball park, the chairs and the tables set in low rows extending as far as the next café, the Coupole. It had an even longer crowded terrace. Opposite the Dôme, on the other corner, was the Rotonde... An intersecting street separated it from the Sélect, which was open all night. We sat at the Coupole. The faces in rows there looked more international, whereas at the Dôme there seemed to be hundreds of recognizable Americans... As it got darker the whole corner seemed to brighten and take on its own exotic life.

*Nowadays most expatriate writers living in Paris avoid the famous cafés of Montparnasse and St-Germain-des-Prés. An exception is Diane Johnson, author of* Le Divorce *and other novels about France. She often frequents the Flore and the Deux Magots. Short-story writer Mavis Gallant told us that writers today do their work at home and tend to patronize their neighborhood cafés, places where they can go without being noticed. But she has also said that she enjoys sitting in the famous Left Bank cafés, eavesdropping on the people near her. Novelist Jake Lamar, author of* Bourgeois Blues *and* Rendezvous Eighteenth, *lives in Montmartre and favors local cafés like the Cépage Montmartrois. He also directed us to Le Rouquet, an appealing cafe near St-Germain-des-Prés. Lamar has mentioned that, living in Paris, he has learned to appreciate "quality of life things [like] sitting in a café on a sunny afternoon." He says in Paris you become more appreciative of the little moments, and that it's a city where "everybody from the baker to the literary critic respects people who write books and care about literature."*

# Les Deux Magots

**Place St-Germain-des-Prés
(01.45.48.55.25)
Métro: St-Germain-des-Prés
Open daily 7:30AM–1:30AM**

*I*n the Deux Magots I could see [F. Scott] Fitzgerald coming to meet me with his elegant and distinguished air," recalled Morley Callaghan in *That Summer in Paris*. The Deux Magots is what most people think of when they imagine a literary café. Named after the two Chinese figures in the main room, in the nineteenth century the Deux Magots was a shop selling Chinese silks.

Later, as a café, Les Deux Magots became a favorite of the intelligentsia, including the poets Rimbaud and Verlaine, André Breton, and other Surrealists. Picasso, Giacometti, and St. Exupéry came here. Hemingway was often seen writing in either the Deux Magots or the Flore.

Prices at the Deux Magots are comparable to those of its neighbor, the Café de Flore. Most tourists tend to prefer the Deux Magots, with its large terrace and expansive corner view. The people-watching on the Place St-Germain-des-Prés is endlessly fascinating.

# Café de Flore

**172 blvd Saint-Germain
(01.45.48.55.26)
Métro: St-Germain-des-Prés
Open daily 7:30AM–1:30AM**

"*The* chief representative of this new energy in artistic circles was a writer, Jean-Paul Sartre, and his headquarters was in a café," wrote James Campbell in *Exiled in Paris*. According to Simone de Beauvoir, although she and Sartre patronized many cafés, the Flore was a particular favorite, the "head-quarters" they usually chose.

"You would see Picasso there, smiling at Dora Marr," wrote Beauvoir, "and Jacques Prévert holding forth to a circle of acquaintances. It always gave me a thrill of pleasure at night to walk in out of the darkness and find myself in this warm, well-lit, snug retreat, with its charming blue and red wallpaper."

The Café de Flore has long been a favorite of intellectuals and writers, French and foreign. James Baldwin wrote much of *Go Tell It On the Mountain* there. Janet Flanner, the *New Yorker* correspondent, recalled in *Paris Was Yesterday* that she would often see Picasso sitting in the Flore with his friends. Jacques Prévert and Albert Camus were regulars. And influential French journalists still meet in the room upstairs.

We had been cool towards the Café de Flore, thinking it overpriced, popular without a particular reason for being so, trading too much on its reputation and historical associations. But we have to admit, there is something appealing about the Flore. On a cold October afternoon early in the week, with hardly a tourist in sight, the Flore is crammed, and by the sound of it, most people are delighted to be here. The 4-euro espresso tastes strong and good, served in the signature green-and-white Café de Flore cups. Add another 3 euros and you get coffee with a trace of Scotch, not a bad idea on a really frigid day.

Of an afternoon, try the smoky ambiance of the Flore, with its Deco lighting, pale walls, warm wood, red moleskin banquettes, and chattering clientele. Young couples meet here; we also noticed a pair of well-dressed women at an afternoon's end, and some prosperous-looking French businessmen. They drink coffee, hot chocolate, small glasses of red wine.

Here are family groups, with many people not looking especially formal. Jeans are the fall uniform of many, regardless of age. Waiters appear in the classic black vest and pants, contrasting with their white shirts, and the spotless long white aprons wrapped around them. A perky black bow tie sets it all off. They rap out loud, clear, precise directions for someone working behind a screen: "Un thé, un!" "Deux chocolats, deux!"

An elderly Frenchman clutches a paperback classic as he edges towards the red banquette that will give him a view of the whole room. The tableful of Italians next to us could be tourists, in fact they must be, judging by the serious picture-taking going on. A mother and her daughter, the daughter with an art student's portfolio, enter and sit near us. They are from near the Place de Clichy, they tell us. Later they share with us their excitement at having just recognized a celebrity, the actor Fabrice Luchini, a stage actor who appeared in the film *La Discrète*.

The Flore is more than a local hangout, more than a stop for a pre-dinner drink. It is an embodiment of the driving energy of Paris; it is clamorous, irresistible—the pulse of a great city.

# Café de la Mairie

**8 Place St. Sulpice, 75006**
**(01.43.26.67.82)**
**Métro: St. Sulpice**
**Open Mon–Sat 7AM–8PM, Sun 9AM–9PM**

This is the local café for one of the world's most desirable neighborhoods: the rich artistic and literary world of the 6th. Some of the great French publishing houses are close by. The Sorbonne is not far. Richard Wright lived nearby on the rue Monsieur le Prince. The Café de la Mairie was well known among older generations of American college students away on their junior year abroad. Many wealthy and famous people, celebrities at least in France, live in the area and consider this their local café. Perhaps you will even catch a glimpse of Catherine Deneuve.

In the morning you may take your coffee outside, almost in the shadow of the great church St. Sulpice, in Paris second in size only to Notre Dame. Often the bells toll as you look out on a small square and a large and exuberant nineteenth-century fountain. The Jardin du Luxembourg is just to the south.

The clientele at this café is definitely upscale. Older women here dress with traditional French elegance. Many of the men have the carefully designed nonchalance of

people who have taken great care about their appearance. Beards are not at all common in most of Paris. Here, they are. The young people at the Café de la Mairie tend to be photogenic, with that bold self-confidence that seems natural only in the young.

There are the classic café props outside: the wicker chairs, the umbrellas, the great plane trees, so distinctive and so French. The Italian motorscooter parked alongside looks like something left over from Audrey Hepburn's *Roman Holiday*. The stiff, black-suited waiter dances among the tables, his tray held perfectly level. The antique and oh-so-Parisian *colonnes Morris*—they're all here. The revolving kiosk bears news and pictures of cinema and theater, and a Corot sky above frames it all.

This important café, on the square for 40 years or more, has its future assured by the look of the many young people who go there of an afternoon and sit with their bottles of Perrier and Coke Light. Out on the front terrace formed by the café's taking over part of the square is a mixture of people: leftists clutching *Le Monde*, retirees with their novels, local business people. All enjoy the cool breezes flowing across the park and across the newly cleaned façade of Saint Sulpice.

Service is offhand but competent—even from the retirees out front the waiter asks for the money for their gin and tonic and glass of rosé as he puts them down. Could it be that the same people have wandered off forgetfully in the past? (Our own bill isn't presented until some time after we've finished our drinks).

But distraction would come easily in such a place, with the beautiful people emerging from the Yves St. Laurent Rive Gauche shop, with the free-flowing fountain in front, the soft, earth tones of the giant columns fronting nearby Saint Sulpice. This is the church F. Scott Fitzgerald refused to enter, telling Morley Callaghan he couldn't, "because once I was a Catholic, you know."

Lithe young things lope past, most wearing the blue jeans that this year are "in." Next year, who knows? The bell from Saint Sulpice summons the faithful to evening prayer—but no one from the Café de la Mairie moves. Finally a clutch of *intellos* (intellectuals) get up to leave, the bearded gentleman having finished his discussion of seventeenth-century Japan. An elderly lady, a lawyer who lives across the way, entertains us with talk of her fight to preserve a building near the square from the developers who'd like to tear it down and put something new in its place. This building, she tells us, is where Tallyrand used to visit his mistress.

# Le Sélect

**99 blvd du Montparnasse, 75006
(01.45.48.38.24)
Métro: Vavin
Open daily Mon–Fri 7AM–2:30AM,
Sat and Sun until 4AM**

My friendship with Hemingway seemed to give us an anchor beyond our own neighborhood. At least once a week I would see him for boxing. Afterwards the two of us would walk up to the Sélect to meet Loretto and have a drink…

By ten in the evening Loretto and I, established at our table at the Sélect, might remain there with friends for hours or we might go to a party. There was always a party…

—Morley Callaghan, *That Summer in Paris*

During the legendary "Crazy Years" of the 1920s, many of the most creative young people from Britain and the United States flocked to Paris. Some of these emigrants would become quite famous and a list of them would be both long and impressive. Americans were able to live cheaply in Paris then, and could get along quite well on a modest income. Many of the young men were soldiers who had survived the Great War and had become disillusioned, cynical, and often aimless—The Lost Generation, they were called, as coined by the writer Gertrude Stein. Paris appealed to them: the French were tolerant; the wine was cheap, the food good, and there were always large groups of fellow expatriates at the favored cafés, some of which, like Le Sélect, stayed open all night.

Most of the legendary Montparnasse cafés made famous by American writers and artists in the '20s have changed beyond recognition. La Rotonde now has the gloomy charm of an all-night New Jersey diner. Le Dôme has become a fancy and expensive restaurant, with a velvet-and-fringe-draped interior that would be considered overdone in Miami Beach. Only Le Sélect would be essentially familiar to the patrons of the prewar period. The sidewalk terrace is still open in all but the worst weather, although now with less sunlight flooding in. Inside, Le Sélect is not all that different from what it was in 1925. This café has been a favorite of American artistic sorts from

Aaron Copland to Allen Ginsberg. Small and somewhat more relaxed than most cafés, Le Sélect brings in people from the neighborhood as well as tourists looking for a bit of history.

Perhaps it's the spirit of the original owners, a couple usually called "Monsieur and Madame Sélect," that has protected the place. They were notoriously difficult, and stories are still told about the customers who clashed with them. Monsieur Sélect once forbade the artist and illustrator Guy Arnoux from being served at his bar, claiming that he provoked fights. Arnoux was unfazed: he continued to sit on the terrace and bribed a waiter to bring him a beer from the Dôme, across the street, which he proceeded to drink in full view of everyone at the café. When Sélect found out, he was naturally furious.

A more serious quarrel arose between Madame Sélect and the poet Hart Crane. He and his friends were celebrating the 4th of July by building castles of the little white saucers that the cafe furnished when one ordered a drink. When a waiter counted his saucers and presented the bill, Crane decided that he was being overcharged and refused to pay Madame Sélect. She called the police. Instead of letting him go with a warning or fine as was usually the case, they kept him in jail for several nights.

In later years, the Sélect became known as a lesbian hangout. Simone de Beauvoir wrote that she and Sartre would go there, sitting "among the crop-haired lesbians, who wore ties and even monocles on occasion; but such exhibitionism struck us as affected."

The Sélect continued to be a writers' café in the 1950s. In his autobiography, the African-American writer Chester Himes mentioned that he would spend the afternoons working there on his novel *A Jealous Man Can't Win*:

> So I quit Alliance Française and devoted all my time to writing… I'd grown a mustache and Marlene and I looked sinister as we walked through the Latin Quarter… ignored by the French childen of Luxembourg Gardens and invisible to the grown-up French on Rue Vavin as we approached the Café Sélect from the back, where I did my writing.

Le Sélect was not built in the avant-garde style of the period, although it has a few Art Deco flourishes. It seems like an older café. The walls are tan, the frosted-glass light fixtures are old, and the ceilings are relatively low. There are three rather small rooms, one with a serious bar. You'll notice that they have a collection of champagnes and a nice selection of single malt whiskeys, and one suspects that they attract a discriminating clientele. The food, though, is simple and not expensive, and unlike in some cafés, it can be surprisingly good. There are always a few posters advertising art exhibitions, most of them long over.

The popular terrace has a southern exposure and, in the days before the high-rise was built across the street over the

Coupole, they say that it received a glorious amount of sunlight. It's still one of the nicer café terraces in Paris.

Much more of a traditional café than most of the others on the standard literary tourist circuit, Le Sélect is smaller and more intimate. It's also quieter, not attracting the noisy and boisterous crowds you find in La Coupole across the street. People actually read newspapers here and some of the people you see might work for them. You can come here and find solitude, especially if you sit inside.

If you go to the Sélect, you'll enjoy the old-fashioned look, the quiet ambiance, the feeling that this is a place where literary history has been made.

# Le Tournon

**18 rue de Tournon, 75006**
**(01.43.26.16.16)**
**RER: Luxembourg**
**Open Mon–Fri 7AM–8PM**
**Closed in July**

To many Americans who came of age in the mid-1950s, Le Tournon was one of the best known of the Parisian cafés, thanks to a feature article in *Life* magazine. The Tournon was described as the gathering spot for an entire generation of African-American writers and artists who had taken up residence in Paris. This was quite extraordinary: up to then the mainstream American press had had little to say about blacks in general and even less about black artists and intellectuals.

The cartoonist Oliver Harrington was one of the stars of the group of black expatriates who gathered at the Tournon, a group that included Richard Wright, Chester Himes, the painter Beauford Delaney, the sculptor Howard Cousins, and sometimes James Baldwin.

In his autobiography *My Life of Absurdity*, Chester Himes described evenings at the Tournon:

> Ollie [Oliver Harrington] became my best friend at the Café Tournon. He was the best raconteur I'd ever known; he kept large audiences entertained and drew people to the Tournon to hear him. We used to keep audiences entranced.

> The proprietors, M. and Mme. Alazar, loved Ollie and he was a sort of accepted leader for all of the blacks of the Quarter, who in turn attracted all the black Americans in the city. It was really Ollie who singlehandedly made the Café Tournon famous in the world.

George Plimpton and others associated with the newly-formed *Paris Review* also settled into the Tournon and made it their unofficial headquarters, but the only literary souvenir today is an old brass plaque commemorating Joseph Roth, an important, although not widely known, Austrian writer. There is no suggestion that Baldwin, Wright, Himes, or for that matter, George Plimpton and his friends were ever here.

In the early and mid 1950s, Le Tournon was patronized more by foreigners than the French. Some people speculated that the French were staying away because the owners, the Alazars, were suspected of having been *collabos* or collaborators during the Occupation. A large photo of Madame Alazar walking with a shaved head and followed by a jeering crowd used to hang behind the bar.

Bavette d'aloyau 11 €
Les desserts Maison
Crumble pommes et poires
Tarte aux Mirabelles
Crème au Caramel

Le Tournon has changed. The pinball machine is gone; drugs are, presumably, no longer sold in the basement; and there's now a highly polished copper bar with drinks for what looks like a wide range of clientele. The French Senate is just down the street, at the entrance to the Jardin du Luxembourg, and Le Tournon attracts its share of expensively-dressed older gentlemen. It also attracts more simply-clad locals, tradesmen, and women who work in nearby shops. One woman brought in her beagle, a dog we hadn't seen much of since the days of Lyndon Johnson. The dog was French and well behaved.

In the 6th, the Tournon is a welcome respite from the glitz of the trendy boutiques. It's a return to the essentials. With its cheap loud colors, formica tables, and neon circle above the bar, which is also decorated with ads for beer, the only hint here of the Tournon's privileged setting is the classy-looking building across the way and the occasional politician who drops in from the Senate.

For a café in such a high-priced area, the Tournon is inexpensive. Coffee and beer are at the lower-priced end of the Parisian café scale, and decent sandwiches cost a little over 2 euros. James Baldwin would have liked that.

· 3 ·

# NEIGHBORHOOD CAFÉS

*To understand Paris, you must sit in a café—perhaps at a sidewalk table beneath lush plane trees facing a broad boulevard or historic square... You must let the sense of the city soak in. Above all, you must take your time. The hours spent at a café—hours of watching, thinking, idling—aren't wasted. They're part of the ebb and flow of the French day, giving it rhythm and meaning.*

*—Angela Mason, "Coffee or Killing Time"*

*Usually an unpretentious place no one pays much attention to, the neighborhood café can be the Parisian café at its best. It's the ideal spot for escaping from your apartment or hotel, for taking the measure of your surroundings, meeting a friend or making a new acquaintance, banishing the gloom of a rainy day, or catching some sun on a clear one. These are the cafés where you're most likely to see Parisians up close, where attractive young people chat each other up, where romance flourishes and the day's news is shared and debated. There's a modesty, an understated quality about these cafés. Some you happen upon by chance, and you find that bonhomie, that good-humored welcome that's rather special and keeps you coming back.*

*When you ask Parisians about their favorite café, it's invariably a neighborhood one, close to work or home. Often they can't quite recall the name, but remember exactly how to get there. You may not have enough French to chat with the proprietor of your local bakery; the checkout clerk at the supermarket usually has no time to talk—but the man or woman behind the bar of your local café, if not too rushed, will make an effort to communicate with you. That human contact is what makes a large city warm and unforgettable.*

*The following cafés are listed by neighborhood. Some happen to be modest cafés in fashionable settings; others, like the Bar des Théâtres, fit in perfectly with their surroundings.*

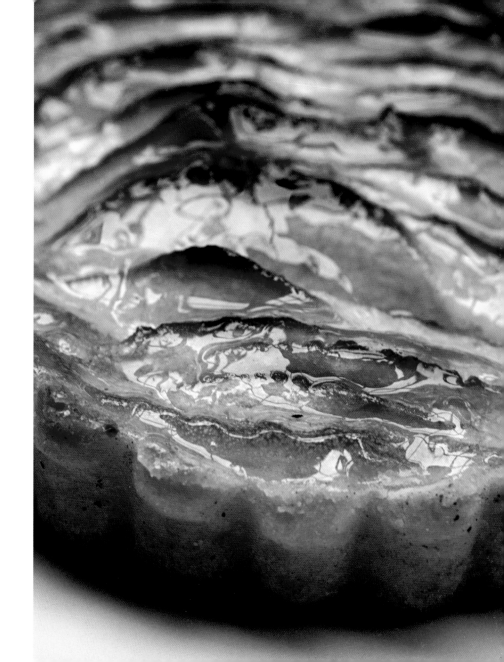

## RIGHT BANK
### CHAMPS-ELYSÉES

# Bar des Théâtres

**6 ave Montaigne, 75008 (01.47.23.34.63); Métro: Alma Marceau. Open daily 9AM–2AM**

The avenue Montaigne is the most expensive residential street in Paris. Marlene Dietrich lived here at number twelve. The Plaza Athenée, one of the legendary luxury hotels, is on this avenue. So are the outposts of most of the great fashion houses. Very few cafés are in this expensive neighborhood, but there is one: the Bar des Théâtres. If you've ever dreamed of being in Paris and surrounded by "beautiful people," this is the place where it could indeed happen.

It's across the street from the famous Théâtre des Champs-Elysées, where Diaghilev presented *Les Ballets Russes*. Igor Stravinsky scandalized music lovers there with his new and daring *Rite of Spring*. In 1925 Josephine Baker, dressed in a few feathers, became the toast of Paris with an electrifying first night's performance in *La Revue Nègre*. (Sidney Bechet was also in the company.) Hemingway called Baker "the most sensational woman anyone ever saw." Cole Porter and his friend Gerald Murphy produced a satirical musical and, a few years later, George Antheil shocked *le tout Paris* with his cacophonous *Ballet Mécanique,* in which the mechanical contraptions produced so much wind that a man's toupee blew off.

After performances at the Théâtre, performers and the lively after-show crowds would pour into the Bar des Théâtres. During our last visit, a smiling waitress informed us that this café has been owned by the same family for three generations. The quality of this neighborhood is suggested by a story Art Buchwald tells in *I'll*

*Always Have Paris*, the memoir of his Paris years. He had taken his wife Ann and her mother to dinner at the Plaza Athenée:

> We were the only ones there when Gary Cooper walked in alone. We invited him to join us. A few minutes later, Ingrid Bergman arrived by herself and we invited her to sit down. (Years later it dawned on me that something was going on between Cooper and Bergman.) Then Anatole Litvak, the director, joined us, with Bettina, the model, who was Aly Khan's girlfriend. It was a merry table and we all had a ball, and my mother-in-law was in heaven.

The Bar's location opposite the Théâtre des Champs-Elysées gave us a chance while sipping coffee to admire that building. Its superb Art Deco bas-relief is said to have been inspired by the dancer Isadora Duncan. Our waiter acted very theatrical himself, presenting our *carafe d'eau* with a song on his lips, and later two generous-sized cups of *café allongé*—"café Américain" he called it.

This is the place to see *le tout Paris*, fashionable Paris: the models, the directors, the artsy and "in" folk. If you're ever going to see a deeply-tanned South American billionaire clad in a white silk suit, it will probably be here. A beautiful Asian woman, remote and cool, chain-smoked at a nearby table. The fashion designer and former Chanel model Inès de la Fressange was quoted in the *Los Angeles Times* as saying:

> I always go to the Bar des Théâtres. It's typically French—in the best, not the worst way, with a very Parisian esprit. The waiters are spirituél and funny. They address you as "Princesse" or "President" if you're a man. It's a simple, unassuming place, on the most sophisticated street in the world, the avenue Montaigne. I love that contrast.

The "look" at this café is minimalist. Wall sconces bear the two faces of theater, comic and tragic. There's a glassed-in terrace, with simple modern wooden tables, black and red variations on the classic *Thonet* chair, and posters here and there of theatrical happenings. There's nothing spectacular about the decor, but the location is a draw in itself.

LE MUSÉE DU LOUVRE

# Le Crapaud

**64 rue Jean-Jacques Rousseau, 75001
(01.42.36.14.90)
Métro: Louvre-Rivoli
Open Mon–Sat 7:30AM–2AM**

*I*f you've been looking for Le Gutenberg, this is it. This small café, under new management, has been renamed Le Crapaud (the toad). The new name, although it sounds off-putting to English speakers, means that the café is now adorned with cheery-looking little toads, many in places where you'd least expect them.

Mercifully, Le Crapaud is still the same simple café with an old-fashioned look about it. There's a newly off-white ceiling, and little squares of colorful pastel designs framed here and there for decor. Otherwise nothing has changed.

This could be one of the hundreds of small unpretentious cafés that used to dot the city in the old days. So it becomes all the more important to us now, during the days of the plastic formula makeovers. It's easy to see how Le Crapaud draws in

*Left: Detail of Le Louvre*

workers from the area, employees of France Telecom and the large post office across the street, people who most definitely would not be in Calvin Klein ads. Tourists are uncommon here, although certainly not unwelcome. The coffee is cheap and the wines a good value, especially the big two-fisted wines of the Southwest. There's even a stab at cocktails made from vodka and gin, although so far we've never actually seen anybody drinking one. A pleasant dining room upstairs has an *ardoise* listing inexpensive lunch possibilities.

At the Crapaud almost everyone stands at the bar, and you'll see a cross-section of Parisians, most of whom probably did not attend the Sorbonne. Many look as if they could have wandered out of a prewar Brassaï photograph. Some come in uniforms. We saw one young man with a long and elegant

silk raincoat draped around his shoulders. The barman could be an actor from one of the minor French *policier* films of a few years ago. If the people at the bar don't actually know each other, they talk as if they do.

CIRQUE D'HIVER–RÉPUBLIQUE

## L'Entrée des Artistes

**8 rue de Crussol, 75011**
**(01.48.05.71.25)**
**Métro: Filles du Calvaire or République**
**Open daily 8AM–2AM**

This 'Winter Circus,' still the most popular in all of Paris, seemed to us… a kind of family paradise. We could buy standing room for ten sous… The show unfolded before us like a magic spell, an enchant-ment… After the performance we always went to the stage door on Rue de Crussol where our favorites came out in their ordinary street clothes. We followed them on foot, thrilled to be near them, until they turned in to a little tavern where they went to eat after their strenuous show.

—*Maurice Chevalier,* My Paris

*I*f you happen to be in Paris during the fall or winter, you should consider going to the Cirque d'Hiver, the place where Hemingway would go to box a few rounds with his friends and where young Maurice Chevalier began to dream about going on the stage. After you've seen the show, now more Las Vegas than Ringling Brothers, with its dazzling effects created by lights, live music and accomplished *artistes*, consider stopping at a little café on the rue de Crussol, beside this famous monument.

At the Cirque we asked, "Where do the *artistes* go between shows?" and we were directed towards a small bar, l'Entrée des Artistes. It's not much to look at—simple, with cheap paneling on the walls, and a bar made of chipped beige formica. Yet the welcome is warm, and this is where you're most likely to get a look into the lives of the circus folk.

Almost immediately we found ourselves deep in conversation with two circus people, Max, a musician, and Diane, an assistant. We asked them about the acts we'd just seen: how did anyone ever get cats, doves, and a vulture to work together? How does one persuade a cat to do anything at all? Max replied that the trainer, Julian, had raised the vulture since it was an egg, that he has incredible patience and uses rewards in coaxing the animals to perform.

Surprised to have seen so many beautiful women dancers in a circus, we asked about them. "Well, after all, this is Paris," Max reminded us with a smile. He added a bit of insider information: most of the dancers are actually English. It's been something of a tradition in Paris, ever since the original Bluebells, to hire English dancers. And he speculated that another factor encourages the employment of English women: "They don't fuss so much about the details of their contract. All the French girls think of is their union contract. Ask them to do a little bit more and they go berserk…" and he imitated a screeching woman.

On another visit we chatted with Aziz Ould, who, with his brother Malik, owns l'Entrée des Artistes. The two men are originally from Algeria, and Aziz mentioned that a third of the Paris café-bars are now owned by Kabyles, people from his region. He's friendly, very ready to chat and make customers welcome in this small bar. The brothers have plans to transform l'Entrée—they envision barstools with a circus theme and a large mirror with the café's name on it; they want to get the neon strip around the top of the bar working again or maybe even replace it with a better one. But we like this café just as it is.

PLACE DES VOSGES, MARAIS

# Le Royal Turenne

**24 rue de Turenne, 75004**
**(01.42.72.04.53)**
**Métro: Chemin Vert**
**Open daily 7:30AM–midnight**

Everybody knew the square, with its three cafés: first the café-restaurant on the corner of the rue des Francs Bourgeois, then Le Grand Turenne opposite, and finally, 30 meters away, the Tabac des Vosges.

—*Georges Simenon*

*Left: La Musée Carnavalet*

This café was called Le Grand Turenne in Georges Simenon's detective novel, *L'Amie de Madame Maigret,* although no one in the café seems to be aware of it. (Simenon's Inspector Maigret is the French counterpart of Sherlock Holmes.)

Le Royal Turenne's location is prime, at the intersection of two major streets in the Marais, the Parisian equivalent of Greenwich Village or Chelsea. It's a few feet from the Place des Vosges, the housing built for the nobility in the early 1600s, and near the Musée Picasso and the Musée Carnavalet.

Le Royal Turenne is not a large café, and patrons may wish to sit on the terrace even in cool weather. Large heaters keep everyone warm, so there is the illusion of experiencing winter without discomfort. If you sit inside, you'll notice the walls of light stone, the formica, chrome, and mirrors, as well as the large glass windows.

The pleasant and energetic proprietress, Mme. Florence Raynal, has owned the Royal Turenne since 1999. She's originally from Espalion, a small village in the Auvergne, and she mentioned the challenges facing Auvergnats when they came to Paris and started cafés. In her café you'll be surrounded mainly by a mixture of locals, people who live or work in one of the world's most desirable areas. The tourists who come by could be from anywhere.

La rue des Francs Bourgeois, one of the streets at this corner, is a world center of elite boutiques and avant-garde shops. Strange shoes that are not sold anywhere else can be found here. An Issey Miyake boutique is next to a sandwich shop. Vintage, museum-quality nineteenth-century photographs are sold in a gallery just down the road.

On a recent winter visit, we saw a dignified older man with a copy of *Le Monde,* the intellectual left-wing newspaper, under his arm, rounding the corner on rollerblades and heading north. We don't think anyone else noticed.

PLACE VENDÔME, RITZ HOTEL

# *Le Rubis*

**10 rue du Marché-St. Honoré, 75001 (01.42.61.03.34); Métro: Tuileries.**
**Open Mon–Fri 8AM–10PM, Sat 9AM–3:30PM**

A survivor from an earlier Paris, Le Rubis is a longtime favorite of workers in the select quarter of St. Honoré—the area of Gucci and Maxim's. Not many of the wealthy tourists swinging their designer bags from Louis Vuitton and Hermès would find their way to this modest nineteenth-century corner bar on an obscure side street, but those who work nearby do. Every café serves wine, but Le Rubis is one of the few that have a more serious interest in it and offer many varieties.

Joëlle, the proprietress behind the bar, informs us that Le Rubis, this small and distinctive watering hole in the city center, has been a café since the early 1900s. At first, she says, it was a place "mal famé"—of bad reputation, a hangout for cutthroats. Then in 1948, a man named Gouin opened it as a wine bar.

Nowadays what you see are not cutthroats but respectable-looking French lawyers, businessmen, and tradespeople who come in to stand at the bar. It's the kind of place where older men enter and shake hands with the proprietor much as they've probably done for the last 20 years, where everyone seems to know everyone else, and people talk a lot, sometimes all at the same time. There's talk of politics, of course. These are not the intellectuals of St-Germain-des-Prés, but more ordinary people.

An eccentric Deco shape in curved wood arches over the bar, accented with swirls of pink and white neon lighting. The supporting pillars are a dark shiny red. Small lamps on sconces with large shades provide a warm glow.

Albert Prat, the proprietor, is a pleasant, reserved individual, quietly visiting with the regulars. Between meals this tends to be a men's bar, frequented by men from their early middle years up to the *troisième âge*, or retirement. Their wives or girlfriends, when they appear, are more likely to sit at the plain formica tables that line the wall. A few students turn up, to down a beer or two along with their ever-present cigarettes (no non-smoking tables exist).

The large windows overlook the rue du Marché-St.Honoré, and you shake your head in disbelief at finding this simple café, this jewel without fuss or pretensions, in an area not far from the Place Vendôme and the Louvre.

## GARE DU NORD

# Au Rendez-Vous des Belges

**23 rue de Dunkerque, 75010 (01.42.82.04.72); Métro: Gare du Nord. Always open.**

This café is still the well-loved little hole-in-the-wall opposite the Gare du Nord. It was redecorated in 2000, with a modern brass-colored bar, new banquettes, and murals depicting the owner with his friends. We'd like to see vintage travel posters of some of the destinations of trains from the Gare du Nord, but the wallpaper on the ceiling pictures wine bottles. Au Rendez-Vous des Belges is a rather ordinary-looking little café with an unusual clientele. Where else can you count on hearing train conductors greet each other in Flemish?

The Rendez-Vous des Belges keeps pulling people in: trainmen, tourists, travelers from all over. We noticed an all-male group of sturdy regulars coming in to stand at the bar. We asked them a question: "Why do people associated with the railway, the trainmen, conductors, and those who work in the offices at the SNCF come here instead of going to the Terminus Nord next door?"

"That's too much for the rich—wrong ambiance," one of them replied.
It's true that the Rendez-Vous possesses a coziness, a sense of warm familiarity that not every café-bar can achieve.

Christian, a longtime Paris resident who drives a limousine, told us he stops at the Rendez-Vous des Belges every day. "This is one of the few places where you can meet people from all over," he said. He mentioned the range of the clientele he's noticed: a fair number of Belgians (Flemish is still spoken here), some English people, Dutch, South Americans, and many others.

Madame Vermant, behind the bar, offers her own theories about the success of the place: "We give fast service—people can have a sandwich, a *croque monsieur*, food that's made quickly. Besides there's the ambiance—it's *sympa* and *familiale*."

So the next time you catch the Eurostar for London at the Gare du Nord, instead of grabbing a sandwich in the station from an anonymous vendor, take a look at the Rendez-Vous des Belges. Chances are you'll want to make it your own place for a rendezvous.

PLACE DE CLICHY, NEAR MONTMARTRE

# Le Cyrano

**3 rue Biot, 75017 (01.45.22.53.34); Métro: Place de Clichy. Open Mon–Fri 9AM–2AM, Sat 5PM–2AM**

But Henry [Miller] loved most of all to walk… He soon knew all of Avenue Clichy like the back of his hand… The long sequence of cafés, restaurants, cabarets, movie theaters, residence hotels and twenty-four-hour pharmacies reminded him of that stretch of Broadway between Forty-second and Fifty-third streets. The difference was that Montmartre was even more of a flesh market. With its little dives jammed with prostitutes, pimps, thugs, crooks and other local color, this boulevard at the foot of Sacré Coeur seemed to him the raunchiest corner in all Paris. Vice lurked over everything like an erotic gargoyle.

… Miller also began the habit of doing all his correspondence at cafés… He consumed an enormous quantity of the beverage. Nearly all his letters from this period… carry the letterheads of the cafés around the Place Clichy.

—Brassaï, *Henry Miller: The Paris Years*

While most of Paris is being slowly gentrified and polished, the Place de Clichy, a few blocks north of the St. Lazare railway station, still collects street people and drifters.

There's a fascinating and unusual café, a café with "attitude," just off the Place. It's called the Cyrano, probably in homage to the theaters nearby. Le Cyrano reminds one of 1960s Greenwich Village, or possibly San Francisco. The people who gather are usually young, good-looking in their black leather jackets and jeans. They congregate near the bar—an amazing bar of dark wood in full Art Nouveau curves. You see flowers and leaves in mosaic tiles, the floral shapes surrounded by bits of gold mosaic. You feel miles away from the Starbucks south of St. Lazare. A few older people wander in—one man sits down, lights a cigarette, and fills out a racing form. Henry Miller would fit right in.

Old pastels in large oval frames recall the life of Cyrano de Bergerac. A drinker at the bar has Cyrano's flowing hair and felt cap with a jaunty feather, but his nose does not achieve Cyrano dimensions. Later we notice the same man taking his place with other street people on the concrete steps across the way.

The proprietor, André Camboulas, who also owns Le Tambour, has wisely kept this café much as it was when he found it. This is an old bar frequented by young people. Some of them are from the two theaters in the neighborhood, Le Mary and l'Européen—an actor tells us he stops by quite often.

The mood at Le Cyrano is nostalgic, evoking a fascination with the past. The barmaid plays standards by Piaf and Trenet. Strains of "La Vie en Rose" sound from an old phonograph as we depart.

MONTMARTRE

# Le Cépage Montmartrois

**65 rue Caulaincourt, 75018 (01.46.06.95.15); Métro: Lamarck-Caulaincourt.
Open Sun–Wed 8AM–9PM, Thurs–Sat 8AM–10:30PM**

This neighborhood café is situated in an especially charming part of Montmartre. Seldom visited by outsiders and overlooked even by many Parisians, this residential neighborhood is where the slopes require a bit more effort to climb, the trees seem taller and somehow greener, and the feeling is of a place that has escaped the attention of urban planners. We're not the only ones who like Le Cépage Montmartrois: it's also a favorite of Jake Lamar, formerly with *Time* magazine and now a novelist in Paris. Lamar, who lives nearby, said about Le Cépage, "I go there at least once a week. Sometimes I take my manuscript pages and read over what I've been writing that week." Not a morning person, Jake usually takes advantage of Le Cépage's attractive terrace in the afternoons: "I'll go for a late lunch at about four or five o'clock. [It's] a great place to read or think." He told us that Le Cépage has the right atmosphere, that they can provide excellent *croque-monsieurs*, and that it's not a well-known café—any tourist you do see here probably got lost looking for something else. He mentioned that the clientele includes a "whole range of regular people," construction workers, secretaries on their lunch break, little old ladies, and other people from the *quartier*.

## LEFT BANK
### ST-GERMAIN-DES-PRÉS

# La Charette

**17 rue des Beaux-Arts, 75006 (01.43.25.60.55)**
**Métro: Odéon**
**Open daily 8AM–2PM**

*I*n the morning they were shooting a film in a bistro up near the Place de Clichy, but the people coming into La Charette looked more theatrical by far. No cameras, no makeup needed.

The location is outstanding. La Charette is just down the street from the École des Beaux Arts and right off the rue Bonaparte, in a part of the Left Bank favored by collectors of primitive art and expensive decorative objects. Here you find this honest little café: the clientele, you'd swear, are old-time character actors waiting for the director to show up—although in fact they're probably aging existentialists long ago driven north by the prices at the Deux Magots and the Flore.

Most of the people who come here seem to know each other. The middle-aged men wear old-fashioned jackets, their scarves tied with a careful nonchalance and not needed in this weather. The younger people seem oblivious to anything except each other. They have become friends, probably from attending the art classes down the street.

Posters of ongoing art expositions give a hint of this café's location, and so do the clientele, many of whom come in with portfolios under their arms. We were entertained by the guttural voices of several of the regulars, older men from the neighborhood, including one Walt Whitman look-alike with white hair and a long white beard. He wore the same sort of flat cap favored by MG sports car drivers. Another had his Great Dane lying at his feet, an immense dog that we had to step over, cautiously, to get to our table. These are people you never see at the Big Three cafés, the Deux Magots, the Flore, the Lipp— maybe 40 years ago, but not now.

A long, copper-edged bar has a metal frame for hard-boiled eggs,

*ardoises* listing the latest wine selections in cramped, almost indeci-pherable handwriting, and an old sign: *Ici Pain Poilâne*. The bar is arranged for utility, not beauty: a slew of white porcelain cups are haphazardly piled on the coffee machine, a few apéritifs, whiskies, Ricard, Pernod, stand on sturdy shelves with various sizes of glassware stacked underneath.

Service is businesslike and efficient, prices low. Here is a genuine neighborhood café—but what a neighborhood. Go before it changes.

L'ÉTERNEL BÉNISSANT LE MONDE

DONNÉ PAR S.M. NAPOLEON, III A L'ÉCOLE DES BEAUX ARTS. 1863.

*Above and left: École des Beaux Arts*

## Le Rouquet

**188 blvd St-Germain, 75007**
**(01.45.48.06.93)**
**Métro: St-Germain-des-Prés**
**Open Mon–Sat 7:30AM–9PM**

"Great old Beat poet Ted Joans used to hang out there [at the Rouquet]—he presided there from 4 to 6 PM, Monday, Wednesday, and Friday. His last book was *Teducation*," said Jake Lamar, the American writer and longtime Paris resident who suggested a number of cafés to us. He added: "Le Rouquet is great—and cheap. Nobody knows about it."

When you enter Le Rouquet you feel as if you are going back in time about forty years. You're in a large café on the boulevard St-Germain-des-Prés, not far from the famous church that's the oldest in Paris.

Here you can sit in a literary café that won't charge you 4 or 5 euros for the privilege, unlike the more famous cafés down the street. Real writers could be sitting among the regulars on this terrace, polishing their prose, working out problems in a plot, or taking a break from writing to glance at *Le Monde* or the *Herald Tribune*.

You could be sipping high-priced espresso on the tourist-crowded terraces at the end of the street, where the Flore, the Deux Magots and the Brasserie Lipp dominate, or you could be here, basking in an ambiance that's decidedly retro and

getting a feeling for what the Left Bank scene was like before any of these cafés became too famous, before Sartre and de Beauvoir found the crowds oppressive and had to leave.

Here is mercifully unimproved decor much as it was in the days of Ted Joans and his friends. The walls appear to be plastic imitating marble. The tables are formica replicating burled walnut, the floor a crazy-quilt mosaic tile, much of it cracked. The neon tubes over the bar have sharp angles suggesting lightning, while in the back room they become daisy shapes against cobalt blue.

This part of the Left Bank has high-grade bookshops, one almost next door, and Le Rouquet has always attracted literary people. Others are mesmerized by the wildly distinctive interior design dating from the 1950s, the age of turquoise Cadillacs, tail fins, neon, and Elvis. But most come here, we suspect, to experience a real café, the genuine article, one that hasn't succumbed to the temptations that lurk in the most famous neighborhood of all.

Le Rouquet has a fine, completely glassed-in terrace, and this is where most people sit during the winter. This being Paris and this being the boulevard St-Germain, the people-watching is first rate. It's not to be missed.

ART GALLERIES ON THE RUE DE SEINE

# La Palette

**43 rue de Seine, 75006 (01.43.26.68.15); Métro: Odéon. Open Mon–Sat 8AM–2AM, closed Sundays and holidays**

Well situated on the rue de Seine, La Palette is a favorite of students at the nearby École des Beaux Arts. Inside it's strikingly attractive, with old palettes smeared with dried paint in various colors hanging above the bar, scenes of Paris landmarks painted on pillars and on canvases displayed on the walls, a back room with a dark, century-old air about it, and vintage oil paintings of dubious merit above brown banquettes.

The zinc bar is now edged with copper, a fad that we hope will disappear. It retains an old marble base. There are only two bar stools—most people will stand, or sit in the *salle* or back room.

The service is efficient, possibly a touch brusque: not much effort is put into charming the clientele. And with its location on this exclusive street, lined with art galleries, the Palette can get away with it. Your espresso is thrust in front of you, and then the bar people tend to clump together and start complaining about their day. You see none of the winning smiles and efforts to make conversation you'll find at more typical neighborhood cafés.

Despite its visual charm, La Palette seems a cold place with servers who do their work mechanically and show no signs of welcoming customers. It's not just outsiders that feel this way—a gallery owner down the street told us the same thing. But if you persevere and keep on coming, you may see well-known actors and artists: this is the 6th, after all. Jane Birkin is said to favor this café.

· 4 ·

# CAFÉS BY DESIGN

*For me, designers are quite simply people who put the charm, the wit—in short, a touch of soul—into objects.*
—Andrée Putman, designer

*French design has been influential, if not dominant, for centuries. It is clear that many individual Parisians are visual people, with an unusual flair for style, expressed in hundreds of small details that delight the observer: brilliant displays in shop windows, inspired arrangements of colorful fruits and vegetables in market stalls, the nonchalant elegance with which a Parisienne will knot her scarf. In comparison with English design, the French seems less restrained and more imaginative. Even the Eiffel Tower, now a cliché, was at the time wildly radical, something unprecedented. It could only have been built in Paris.*

*Color is of particular interest to the French. There are certain colors seen only in France, which are subtly different, more appealing than those anywhere else. There is a distinctive blue, it is said, that only Lanvin is allowed to use, and an instantly recognizable Hermès orange. Even a lowly T-shirt from Gaultier, Cacharel, or Kenzo can be in a hue you've never seen before.*

*Art Nouveau flowered in France, and for many people this style is forever identified with the curves and swirls of Hector Guimard's famous métro entrances. Looking back, people recalled a "Golden Age," the Belle Epoque before the First World War. Art Deco, which developed in the 1920s, is also a romantic design, one that makes us think of worldly sophistication, of Noël Coward, of objets d'art of ivory, ebony, and chrome, and of the uneasy combination of cynicism and innocence that marked the period between the two wars. Art Deco started in France and reached its zenith in Paris. It is still wildly popular. The best vintage posters of that period bring extremely high prices, as do the finest examples of Lalique crystal. In contrast to Mucha's lush and sensuous Art Nouveau renderings of Sarah Bernhardt are the more abstract images created a few years later by Paul Colin of the lean and sinuous dancer Josephine Baker. The prewar ocean liner the Normandie, a masterpiece of Art Deco design, is still considered the most splendid ship ever built. The Concorde, although a British and French product, has what people would consider a "French" look, its radical design making it appear more like a mystical white bird than a flying machine.*

Much of the design of the late twentieth century had a strong French influence. The Pompidou Museum—an especially brutal postmodern building, virtually turned inside out to expose the ducts and vents, accentuated in primary colors for all to see—was the first major example of a radical new architecture that has had reverberations in cities as far away as Minneapolis.

Modern French interior design carries on this tradition of audacity and daring. Some important cafés offer sleek styling, using much stainless steel, heavy glass, and halogen lighting. Several of the newest cafés could serve as sets for science fiction films.

If you're interested in design, you may want something other than the typical corner café. The basic zinc bar, the hissing coffee machine, the Thonet chairs, the terrasse—you've seen them before. They're classics, they're good, but they just don't excite.

For the times when you feel like seeing something quite out of the ordinary——and the French are good at creating enchanting places—we propose something different. Some of our choices are cafés with a difference; a few may not even be immediately recognizable as cafés. You will be treated to examples of great French design, and design is an area where the French excel. The world has been imitating them in this ever since they created Versailles and set a standard for glorious interiors.

So prepare to be dazzled.

# Atelier Renault

**53 avenue des Champs-Elysées, 75008**
**(01.49.53.70.70)**
**Métro: George V**
**Open daily noon–1AM**

There are many cafés on the Champs-Elysées, including one of the most famous, Fouquet's, a legend and a refuge for movie stars, Arab princes, and minor royalty.

But we have to admire the ultra-sleek opulence of the café in the Renault showplace. *Atelier* is the French word for workshop, but it's clear that Renault doesn't make cars here. They don't sell them here either. This is a place where the "concept" cars, the dream cars, the prototypes, and, on some occasions, the rare old classics, are displayed.

It's worth a trip upstairs to try the café-restaurant. The decoration is stunning: avant-garde, unexpected, done without regard for expense. Picture a flood-lit café space on metal platforms suspended high above the main floor by thick steel cables. The lights far above remind one of stage lighting. Stainless steel and brushed aluminum are everywhere, and the chairs look like 22nd-century bishops' chairs from some far-in-the-future church.

Young people tend the bar and serve drinks and snacks, and considering the space they have to cover, their youthful energy is needed. The warm and cordial service is a welcome contrast to the somewhat intimidating and futuristic space of cold steel and high-tech design.

# Café Beaubourg

**43 rue St. Merri, 75004**
**(01.48.87.63.96)**
**Métro: Rambuteau**
**Open Sun–Wed 8AM–1AM,**
**Thurs–Sat 8AM–2AM**

"*I* often write at the Café Beaubourg… which I find airy and calm although there's always something to see," wrote the American author Edmund White in *Our Paris*. "All the waiters know Fred [White's Bassett hound] and automatically serve him a croissant in the morning and a bowl of water on a hot day. Despite an inherent discretion, they will sometimes point out the famous people…. In casing the balcony we learned that the tabletops were all painted by celebrated French artists but not signed lest they be stolen." In the same essay White mentioned that the waiters have told him a psychiatrist comes regularly to see his patients there at a table in the café.

The Beaubourg is what the French would call a *café design*, a designer's café: smart, sleek, elegant. Much like the people who crowd its terrace and sit on the designer chairs.

Created by architect Christian de Portzamparc in the late 1980s for Gilbert and Jean-Louis Costes, Le Beaubourg is starkly modern, almost drained of any color. But the design is pure: it has a great expanse of white marble floor, matching black-and-white marble tables, and even, while we were there, a black and white dog, which trotted up to the mezzanine and back down again like a model at a fashion show.

The interior is a welcome change from the hurly-burly of the Place Beaubourg, with its noisy, jostling crowds and the brutal post-modern architecture of the Musée Pompidou. A formidable concrete staircase curves up to an elegantly fenced-in mezzanine, as if we were on the first-class deck on an ocean liner. All that's needed are seagulls and waves outside, but the Pompidou's huge white air-conditioning funnels carry on a nautical feeling. An Art Deco flavor is very much in evidence here, hinting of the French liner *Normandie* and the great days of Cunard. The whimsical chairs remind us of Dali's *Mae West* sofa.

This is a real café, not a restaurant. It offers hors d'oeuvres and light main dishes for the famished, but the slender menu features drinks, which can be ordered at any time.

The Café Beaubourg is relatively expensive for this *quartier populaire*, and the people who come here look cosmopolitan and artistic. The sleek young servers have the sense of style and movement of actors, as some of them may well be. Many of both the patrons and the waiters tend to favor black, although a dapper young man in an immaculate white suit entered just as we were leaving. A middle-aged woman came in with a streamlined gray dog, probably a whippet, but in general, the look here is more Gaultier than Gucci.

## Bricolo Café

**52 rue de Rivoli, (basement of BHV department store), 75004 (01.42.74.90.00); Métro: Hôtel de Ville. Open Mon–Sat 9:30AM–7:30PM, Wed & Thurs until 8:30PM**

The BHV (Bazar de l'Hôtel de Ville) is an otherwise ordinary Parisian department store near l'Hôtel de Ville. What makes it stand out above the others is the basement, which houses one of the world's great hardware stores. If you want a choice of several dozen brass doorknobs, you'll find them here. Gadgets, washers, screws, shoe-repair devices, shelving, sheet metal by the meter, iron, steel and aluminum rods, stoves, garden supplies, wine cellar fixtures, all sorts of chains, cables, and wires—in short, here is everything you could possibly want or need. It's an area that *bricoleurs* (do-it-yourselfers) find fascinating, and others find noisy, crowded, and oppressive.

But even if you're not handy with tools and don't particularly want to be, take a look at the Bricolo Café. It's tucked off to the side in the basement of the BHV. Here is an elaborate stage setting for one of the world's most unusual cafés. Upon entering the Bricolo you feel as if you might have wandered into the distant past, into the basement workshop of a beloved uncle or grandfather, a master craftsman who couldn't bear to throw anything away, who collected old wood and metalworking tools of all descriptions and left them neatly arranged on shelves against the dingy walls. Screwdrivers, vises, and saws are displayed as they would be in a true shop. Paint is peeling picturesquely from an old door on which are mounted wrenches of various sizes, handsaws, files. A vintage drill is set up on a workbench. Tables and chairs look weather-beaten and shabby but are all the more appealing for it.

The setting here rises to the level of theater. You see antique lanterns, once carried to cast a dim light at milking time in barns before the age of electricity. Old metal barstools crowd up against metal-topped tables the color of vintage pewter. The floors are broad, well-weathered planks—or they're cleverly painted to seem that way.

Ignore the computer in the corner, the cash register behind the counter; concentrate on the friendly distressed surfaces of the tables and bar. Hot and cold drinks are served with a smile, and snacks include large slices of fruit tarts. In the morning you can come in for a coffee-croissant breakfast. The coffee is delicious Lavazza and everything is fairly priced.

Unlike the tumultuous BHV basement, filled with confused and frustrated shoppers, the Bricolo Cafe provides an oasis of quiet. Le Bricolo looks ancient, venerable, authentic, and you think you can almost smell the grease and dirt from not only the pre-World War II period but also from before World War I. It's all an illusion; nothing is what it appears to be—the café is relatively new, neat, and very clean.

# Les Gaufres

**Jardin du Luxembourg, 75006**
**(01.43.26.13.65)**
**Métro: Odéon. RER: Luxembourg**
**Open daily 9AM–6:30PM. No credit cards.**

On a sunny summer day this is surely the most romantic spot in Paris. On a rainy day in February it still is. Imagine a tree-lined alley leading to a house in the woods, surrounded by old-fashioned French lawn chairs and little round tables, all in the retro green that goes perfectly with the moss on the trees and the pebbles underfoot.

Every country seems to have its distinctive colors, and the colors of France are more sophisticated than most. The colors at Les Gaufres are retro, and the view is reminiscent of the 1950s. One can imagine this scene in black and white. Tables and chairs are a faded olive green; the pavilion is a dark *vert wagon*, the color of old railway cars. Think of the Orient Express.

Serious-looking scholars from the Senate; white-haired intellectuals; students young and old; dandies in velvet jackets; Parisiennes with hair dyed that peculiar shade of dark red that is only to be found in this city; intense, long-haired girls, black sweaters accentuating their thin figures, huddled together in earnest conversation. Some of the costumes we see here are impossibly romantic: before us is a woman no longer young, her hair cascading down over a black opera cloak covering a burgundy dress.

We hear rapid conversations in French, and a few in English (the 6th is a tourist favorite). The waiter in his signature black-and-white uniform makes a valiant effort to tempt the customers: "Pâtisserie? Cake?" But he finds few takers for anything but a drink. "Café, Mademoiselle?" "Deux cafés, ou deux cognacs?" Our portly waiter rushes about like a character from a Feydeau farce. He seems abrupt but well meaning, reluctant to take the time to puzzle out an order before he runs off to tend another table.

Our hot chocolate in a large porcelain cup is close to perfection. Made with an abundance of bittersweet chocolate, it's just right for a chilly day, something to savor as we look at the fountain and the alley of the queens. If you ever want to arrange a rendezvous with someone in the Luxembourg Gardens, it would be easy to suggest meeting by one of the queens—Mary Stuart, perhaps, or poor Marie Antoinette.

Elderly little Parisiennes perch on the park chairs, or, more daringly, sit on one and extend a tired leg over another. More women are seen in slacks these autumn afternoons. Happily there's relief from the omnipresent cell phones—people at the Luxembourg Gardens don't have them, have turned them off, or are here to escape such modern annoyances.

For a little while life seems to have slowed down. You're left contemplating the tranquility of the park, its groomed shrubs, stone pilasters, the light filtering down through tall trees, and the pigeons that hop by in the shade of evenly-spaced shrubbery. There are potted oleander and palms, the flora of the South. Contrived? Yes. But here, it works.

The café resembles a cast-iron gazebo trimmed with lattice work, its interior an unlikely shade of hot orange. The menus are posted outside—who would be indoors on a day like this? The graceful bandshell nearby has sheltered many musicians, both inexperienced and accomplished.

People come for the drinks and the light lunches, and sometimes they're alarmed to find that credit cards are not accepted. But it seems perfectly in keeping with the Old World atmosphere of this shelter in the park, like Hansel and Gretel's small house in the woods. The Luxembourg Gardens are surrounded by some of the most elegant apartment buildings in Paris, but here one has a feeling of escape from the city. Almost everyone looks as if they've found their secret place, their happy discovery.

# Publicis Drugstore

**La Brasserie, 133 ave des Champs-Elysées, 75008 (01.44.43.79.00);
Métro: Etoile. Open daily, Mon–Fri 8AM–2AM, Sat and Sun 10AM–2AM**

Brigitte Bardot and Jane Birken come here. The late music mogul Eddie Barclay used to stop by. Famous athletes and other celebrities still show up from time to time.

This does not surprise us at all: Le Drugstore is breathtaking. Reopened in 2004, it has a space-age look and a privileged address at the very top of the Champs-Elysées, almost in the shadow of the great Arc de Triomphe. But while the Arc is all about the past and the victories of Napoleon, the Drugstore is a joyous and optimistic celebration of the future. To our left and in front an expanse of glass gives an almost unrestricted view of the Champs-Elysées.

When seated inside, you see metal supports like the struts of a circus tent, an elaborate creation of glass, with complicated and whimsical lighting and an extraordinary bar in the center of the room. The bar itself—clearly inspired by the works of René Lalique—is formed from layers of thick glass, with impressions of icicles and the fanciful shapes formed by frost on a windowpane in winter. A line of little lights gleams under the heavy glass on the sides—lights that can change in color, a waiter informed us. At the bar's center, liqueurs, wine bottles, and gleaming wine and champagne glasses are displayed on shelves of frosted glass.

The room is cool in pale grays and indigo blues. Seating is comfortable and stylish too, with low designer chairs and elegant circular tables in soft gray set against the banquettes in black.

No wonder the wealthy and famous people who live in the area choose this place to stop for a drink, a snack, a prescription: Le Drugstore has it all.

## · 5 ·

# A NINETEENTH-CENTURY LOOK

*I continued up the street to the Boulevard Saint-Michel, where thirst and curiosity prompted me to stop in at a café I had once known. Since I had last seen it... the place had been sold and the new boss had called in a decorator to slick it up, turning the pleasant, easygoing, old-style French café into a restaurant de luxe—a cocktail lounge on Route 4 in New Jersey.*

—A. J. Liebling, *Liebling Abroad*

*T*he Parisian café is one of those images that has entered the imagination of almost every person in the Western world, and the cafés we picture are invariably from the past. Some of them are glorious—the Café de la Paix comes to mind—but most are modest, and like A. J. Liebling, we would be upset to see any change in them. Postwar America had an infatuation with everything French. In the romantic musical An American in Paris Gene Kelly and Leslie Caron dance in old Paris to the incomparable music of George Gershwin. Films made with Paris as a setting invariably included café scenes, but only with classic cafés, lacking views of the Musée Pompidou or the Montparnasse tower or anything that could upset our usual notion of what Paris is supposed to look like. In the film Amélie, cars were digitally removed from the streets to create an idealized, old-fashioned Montmartre.

Paris has been an enchanted city for hundreds of years and has become the world's most popular destination. People go there not only for its sheer beauty, but to experience a life more immediate, more sensuous, more poetic, more tolerant, and, perhaps, more rational. Much of this is illusion, of course, but we sense that there might well be another way of living. One can imagine a home there, something one does not feel as strongly in Berlin, Rome, or Tokyo. France, like the United States, has traditionally thought of itself as the ultimate refuge (although it fills this role much less today than in the past). We hear the echo of Thomas Jefferson's famous saying, "Every man has two countries, his own and France." We go to Paris in an attempt to recapture our idealized picture of the past and to discover who we are.

To most people, Paris is essentially a nineteenth-century city, and that's really the city they want to see. The French love to play with radical change, but at heart they're a deeply conservative people, and fortunately, the core of Paris, the area where tourists stay, remains essentially unchanged. We search for this old city, a place remembered from a hundred famous paintings: misty images by the Impressionists in soft focus, women in long skirts against a *backdrop of majestic buildings near the Opéra, John Singer Sargent's elegant couple strolling in the Luxembourg Gardens, Toulouse-Lautrec's dancers celebrating life in a Montmartre cabaret, Utrillo's views of tranquil village streets.*

*In* Paris was Our Mistress, *when Samuel Putnam recalls his Paris years, the cafés are part of his first impressions of the city:*

> [W]e were fortunate in our initiation: the Tuileries by moonlight, Paris at its loveliest… above all, Paris in the early hours of the morning, an awakening Paris, the honk of Parisian taxis which only Gershwin has captured, the rumble of carts and hoofs over the cobbles, the imperialism of small shopkeepers annexing the sidewalk for their displays, little tobacco shops… the *bistros*, the chauffeurs and *ouvriers* stopping for a morning drink on their way to work, the flower vendors, the kiosks with the world news flaming at one in headlines, the rapidly filling cafés and café terraces . . .

*We suggest that you visit a few cafés that have what we consider a nineteenth-century look. Some are in buildings that are much older than that (Le Temps des Cerises, in the Marais, is beside a building that dates from the early seventeenth century), and a few may have only been cafés for several decades or less. But in them you recall a nostalgia suggested by old photographs of long ago.*

# Café Antoine

**17 rue de la Fontaine, 75016 (01.40.50.14.30); Métro: Jasmin. Open Mon–Sat 7:30AM–11PM**

A hard-to-find jewel in the 16th near Radio France, the Café Antoine remains a café between 3:00PM and 6:30. You can go then just to enjoy a drink and at the same time to admire a small masterpiece. Otherwise this is a restaurant, as it has to be to generate enough income to keep the doors open.

Crusty old men come in and lean on the old zinc bar, a bar that has a fine Empire-style base. But what catches your attention are the tiles on the floor—authentic Art Nouveau, as fine and swirly as they come. It's all by Hector Guimard, the architect responsible for the original Métro entrances and for the extraordinary building, Castel Béranger, down the street.

Antoine is a "transition" café, not pure Art Nouveau, not really Belle Epoque. There's an Art Nouveau façade, an interior with *fin-de-siècle* molding around the ceiling, wall tiles that are an explosion of stylized roses and ribbons, and then the extraordinary floor.

The ceiling is a glass wonder painted with clouds and edged with scrolls, reminding us of certain elaborate *boulangeries* from the turn of the century. Beside us on the wall is a scene of a steeplechase, with horses vaulting over fences, and behind the bar is a similar mural showing a scene along the Marne.

We learn that there have been only three proprietors since the café was built in 1911. The present owner told us he wants to have the whole establishment declared a *monument classé*—currently only the façade is protected—but, as he said, "It's a long process with a lot of paperwork."

# Bar de l'Entracte

**47 rue Montpensier, 75001
(01.42.97.57.76)
Métro: Palais Royal
Open daily 10AM–2AM**

*I*n the Palais Royal area at 17 rue de Beaujolais, you can peer over some café curtains and see where there was once a fashionable and elegant café from the eighteenth century, the Café de Chartres. It's still fashionable, but it's now Le Grand Véfour, a three-star restaurant.

Only a few steps away, but a world away in spirit, is l'Entracte, a tiny old café tucked into the corner of rue Beaujolais and the rue Montpensier. There has been a café at this spot for well over a century.

It is well named "The Intermission," a popular name for cafés near theaters in Paris. Actors and theatergoers from the Comédie Française and the Théâtre du Palais-Royal frequent this place. "When do they show up?" we ask the barmaid. "Avant le spectacle pour manger," she offers, "Après, pour boire." (Before the show, to eat. Afterwards, to drink.)

This is a priceless little nook, with exposed stone walls that seem ancient, a curved Deco bar, and a dusky cream ceiling spotted with modest circular light fixtures. For

serious diners or larger groups, there's a room downstairs with low vaulted ceilings, stone arches, and walls carved out of the rock foundation. Surprisingly, hidden off to the side is a modern kitchen in stainless steel.

A few tiny tables are available outside and in, but most people would rather crowd together at the bar and talk of politics or drama. Signs on the wall suggest what actors and their audience might drink: for holiday celebrations there's Champagne Lanson for the top-liners or a more modest sparkling wine, *Crémant du Loire,* for supporting players or stagehands.

The only other customer on this quiet afternoon was a man who, as he sat studying a playbook, looked as if he might well be in the theater himself.

# *Au Petit Fer à Cheval*

**30 rue Vieille du Temple, 75004
(01.42.72.47.47)
Métro: St. Paul or Hôtel de Ville
Open daily 9AM–2AM**

*I*f you're looking for Old Paris, the Marais is a good place to start. The streets here wind sinuously through the old marsh area. Around you are the small, human-scale buildings of three or four stories, a few still crumbling in disrepair, but most carefully restored and sandblasted clean. This is like the Paris of the eighteenth-century, a *quartier* so ill adapted to motor transport that you marvel every time a bus or large car makes its way down the narrow thoroughfare.

Almost certainly one of the smaller cafés in Paris, Au Petit Fer à Cheval is also one of the most appealing. It's clean, quirky, and uncommon. The Second

Empire bar alone could be a classified monument, with its rich, dark reddish-brown mahogany base, the *fer à cheval* (horseshoe) shape topped in gray marble. For years this has been a traditional stop for the young, the gay, and the artistic—and they're not always the same people.

We enter a small room, made even smaller by the massive bar. This café is old. Nothing much has changed since its opening in 1903. The main room is smoky tan, and is dominated by the bar and an oversized French Empire chandelier, which, surprisingly, doesn't look at all out of place. A large old clock, an hour fast for half of the year, juts out of the wall at one side. There's a charming, fanciful floor in mosaic tile, curving and swirling in patterns under our feet. A vintage movie poster, *La Jument Verte* (The Green Mare), and the immense mirror beside it fill a wall. Seated in the corner, we take in the superb old-fashioned façade, the long narrow doors with heavy antique fittings.

There's a good feeling here. We notice the friendliness when we ask a question: is the singer we're hearing Blossom Dearie? The waiter didn't know, but two people at the bar did—one even passed us a note with the correct spelling of the singer's name, Lise Ekdel. Like other famous cafes and bars, Au Petit Fer à Cheval attracts its share of Anglophones, even in a year when the French are bewailing a lack of English-speaking tourists.

Somehow, walking by on previous visits, we couldn't imagine what all the fuss was about: why should this small café—well situated but with seemingly little else to recommend it—always be crammed full, often overflowing almost onto the street? Now we realize what the Petit Fer à Cheval has going for it: a friendliness, an openness. This is a place where you could get to know the French.

And there are the mirrors, the chandelier, the old train station clock, the array of bottles, and espresso machine separating us from the back room, a room where the seats look like métro benches from the 1950s. The simple white tiles on the walls are also old.

Au Petit Fer à Cheval is the real thing, a one-of-a-kind place, a sentimental favorite, and a part of prewar Paris.

# Le Temps des Cerises

**31 rue de la Cerisaie, 75004
(01.42.72.08.63)
Métro: Sully-Morland or Bastille
Open Mon–Fri 7:30ᴀᴍ– 8:30ᴘᴍ
Closed weekends, holidays, and in
August**

For many years one of our own favorite cafés has been Le Temps des Cerises, a tiny one-and-a-half-story house in the Marais. It's a most unlikely place in an expensive area. We were once told that being part of the former convent of the Celestins, it escaped demolition and is now a classified monument. One would expect to see a café like this in a country village, not near the center of a major city.

As long as we can remember, it had been owned by the Vimards, a couple of great warmth and charm: he with a handlebar mustache and a theatrical flair, she the sensible and down-to-earth counterpart. Before their time, the Temps des Cerises, a café since 1910, was called Trains Bonnet. It was named for Louis Bonnet, who founded the newspaper *L'Auvergnat de Paris,* with its offices next door. Bonnet encouraged people to come to Paris from the Auvergne by the trainload, so the café was known as Trains Bonnet. His newspaper helped Auvergnats to adjust to the capital city; it reduced their sense of isolation and combatted prejudices against them.

On a recent stop we found a different couple, Yves and Michele, in charge. Yves is artistic looking, with a small beard. Michele, pert and pretty, moves with the grace of a dancer. We also noticed a younger clientele than usual, a mixture of people from the area, and we asked Yves who comes to Le Temps des Cerises these days.

"Il y a un peu de tout," explained Yves, "des jeunes, des journalistes, des commerçants du quartier, des ouvriers, des touristes." (A little of everything—journalists, shopkeepers, workers, tourists.)

He told us how, perhaps due to the space limitations, a real mingling takes place—*chefs d'entreprise* (executives) might find themselves chatting with retirees. He added that Michele likes to place people next to each other so that they have a chance to get acquainted over lunch or a drink.

Yves mentioned the École Massillon down the street, educating children from English, German, and Italian families. Frequently their parents stop at the Temps after dropping their children off at school or picking them up in the afternoon—and so for a while, he told us, the café is rather like a little United Nations.

We asked Yves what led him and Michele to invest in the café in the first place. He said they'd gone past and found that Le Temps was for sale. They'd looked around, and been immediately drawn by its charm. "There's something about the house," Yves said, "a feeling, something you can't really define, something wholesome and good."

Previously Yves had worked at a brasserie in Montmartre. Michele made fashion accessories, elegant small purses, from photographic film. Now all of their attention is focused on Le Temps des Cerises. If you're fortunate, you might get a chance to catch an evening, usually once a month, when they arrange for you to hear traditional French folk music there.

# La Patache

**60 rue de Lancry, 75010 (01.42.08.14.35); Métro: République or Jacques Bonsergent. Open daily 6PM–2AM**

Here you have the feeling of gingerly stepping into an old sepia photograph. La Patache could well be an authentic working-class café from the nineteenth century. An old-fashioned coal stove is still used for heat in the winter. It sits in the center of the main room, its pipes snaking up and around along the ceiling, recalling La Patache's past as a real *café-bougnat*, a place where the owner maintained a café and sold coal—a tradition in the Paris café world.

Otherwise, this room is an inspired, impulsive mishmash, with old and faded reproductions of famous art, framed and unframed photos, and mismatched light fixtures of frosted glass. Half of the light bulbs are burned out. Various types of caps and hats are perched incongruously behind the bar. Discolored by time and tobacco, the room is a hundred shades of brown, including all of those colors included in the expensive wax crayon sets of one's childhood: burnt sienna, Indian red, chocolate, taupe.

Reportedly an austere man, Vito, the proprietor, summoned up a half smile and brought our *demis* with dispatch. (But he refused to serve coffee to some young people who asked for it—possibly the coffee machine is out of order.)

La Patache is a bit of a dive, where the regulars look like suspects in a police lineup. On one evening the bar was dominated by a man in a rumpled tweed suit, his long gray locks falling to his shoulders. He struck up a conversation with whoever happened to stand beside him. Otherwise, most of the clientele is young. Many have left scraps of paper with obscure scribblings and cryptic verse in the tin cans on the tables. (You might find one that has something to say to you.) Two girls, each with ponytails and black sweaters, were engrossed in the sort of intense conversation the French seem to love. In the back the *toilettes* (of the old-fashioned variety commonly referred to as Turkish) have affectionate graffitti scrawled around on the walls and door: "If alcohol preserves, M. Vito will last at least 700 years and the Patache too," says one.

If Che Guevara had chosen to spend his exile in Paris, he'd have hung out at the Patache.

## La Renaissance

**112 rue Championnet, 75018 (01.46.06.01.76); Métro: Jules-Joffren. Open Mon–Sat 10AM–midnight**

This is Montmartre, but not the famous part where tourist buses clog the streets and sidewalk artists sketch your image. This is the other side of the hill, a place where foreigners seldom venture, but which is nevertheless attractive, with the flavor of a small provincial city.

La Renaissance was built in 1904 at the height of the Art Nouveau movement, and most of it looks unchanged, steeped in nostalgia and early Parisian style. Much of the decoration is Art Nouveau, but here we see it in an authentic working-class café, not as a reconstruction in a museum. The long bar is curved, the walls are adorned with what is probably the original brown paint. The lights over the bar are, of all things, fluorescent, but they're covered by stained glass shades and are so dim they shed an almost mystical glow. It's *film noir* brought to life in the twenty-first century. It's Orson Welles and *A Touch of Evil* set in Paris, but the Renaissance is a friendly place, not a frightening one. The music, which included some early Miles Davis, was just right.

"I fell in love," admitted Robert Abbas, the owner. "In 1987 I saw the café was for sale and I fell for it—*un coup de coeur*. I told myself, 'It's beautiful, I have to buy it.'"

Small wonder. Filmmakers fall in love with the interior all the time: Sam Shepard played a scene there in *Le Voyageur* (*Homo Faber* in English). It was used in the French films *La Croisiere* and *Les Ripoux* and was a setting for a Franco-American made-for-TV film.

Monsieur Abbas had never previously owned a café. Before taking on the responsibilities of a café-bistro, he'd worked in the textile trade, selling fabric wholesale near Sentier, the garment district. Running a café, he concedes, is extremely hard work, but he appears content.

Sitting in La Renaissance, you can see what he's talking about: the great old curved marble bar from the late 1930s, its semicircle defining the room; original Art Nouveau tiles; enormous mirrors with sensuous curving lines in frosted glass, reminiscent of a Mucha poster; the old ceiling with ochre flaring into burnt orange on the edges. (Fortunately M. Abbas did not have it repainted when he took over.) An antique icebox, solid and massive with sturdy metal fittings, guards a corner.

The ambiance of the Renaissance keeps people coming back. During the day, office workers stop for a coffee or lunch. In the evenings, young people meet up with their friends. Although the first room is a café, the second one is like an old-fashioned bistro, with the classic rails behind the banquettes for hats, scarves, and umbrellas.

At lunchtime everybody is in a hurry: large, appetizing platefuls of the daily special—today it's *blanquette de veau*—are whisked out to the main dining room on our left. The intense and critical French clientele are getting their money's worth and more.

We talk with Aurélien Abbas, the proprietor's son, about his take on the place. Slender, dark-haired, blessed with his father's good looks, Aurélien hesitates in his

attempt to explain his feelings about the Renaissance. Finally he insists that this bistro has *une âme*, a spirit, a soul of its own. How would he describe the Renaissance's "soul"? "Conviviale, historique, avec une empreinte des poètes" he says—it's welcoming, historic, poetic. It's also "un lieu calme pour écrire"—a tranquil place for writing. Writers and directors come here, he tells us.

Nothing has been done to add to or take away from the Renaissance's essential character. And that's the point: nothing has been tampered with or altered in any obvious way. Filmmakers can see that, and that's why they keep coming.

As we were leaving La Renaissance, we asked Robert Abbas if we could take a last photo, in the dining room this time. He glanced around and returned to us, looking a little uneasy. "Better not," he said, adding, with a conspiratorial smile: "I think there are people here who are not lunching with their wives."

## · 6 ·

# A GATHERING OF THE YOUNG

*I was attracted to the Left Bank, south of Notre Dame. The Sorbonne was there, and so many young students. The cafés hummed with literary and philosophical conversations. There was jazz and dancing and small boîtes where you applauded by snapping your fingers... The ghosts of Hemingway and George Orwell lurked around corners...*

—Peter Miller, *The First Time I Saw Paris*

*S*ometimes *people ask how we find the latest* cafés-branchés, *the places currently popular with young people. Once it happened like this: some time ago we were dining at a fashionable new bistro near the Seine, the kind of place favored by mid-level foreign businessmen on limited expense accounts. Our waiter looked as if he might be aware of the latest trends, so we asked him where young people were going. He suggested that we take a look at the cafés around the Place Sainte Marthe, an area we'd heard of but had never visited.*

*We found the Place Sainte Marthe in a part of Paris where tourists seldom go, a* quartier populaire, *or working-class area, known as Belleville. This is not the Paris of elegance and romance, of picture postcards and 5-euro cups of coffee. Belleville is comparable to the immigrant sections of Queens or the East End of London. Cars here have unrepaired dents. On some buildings you see partially torn posters publicizing long-ago demonstrations. Even the cats have a wild and wily look. At cafés you're more likely to see a plastic helmet slung over a chair than a Burberry raincoat. But we found lively cafés on this square.*

*Not all of the cafés where the young get together are found in poorer areas like Belleville. The Café de l'Industrie, for example, is in the more prosperous part of the 11th, near the Bastille. And one could say that Au Petit Fer à Cheval in the ultra-fashionable Marais (mentioned in Chapter V: A Nineteenth-Century Look) draws a younger crowd.*

*If you go to one of these cafés, don't be afraid to ask the people next to you for their recommendations—many Parisians enjoy talking about their city and sharing their favorites. (Most French people who are thirty and younger have probably studied some English.)*

*If you have fears that the French café might be going under, that it's on the brink of collapse due to competition from the lower-taxed fast-food outlets or sleek, well-financed American imports, think again. Go and see these real cafés that have what it takes to bring in the young.*

## Café Banal

**39 blvd du Port Royal, 75013
(01.43.31.27.39); Métro: Gobelins
Open Mon–Fri 10AM–10PM**

The Café Banal is anything but. It's a student hangout of high intensity, high density, high testosterone, and low prices. Not much has been spent here on appearances: try to imagine a low point in uninspired 1950s design, with ugly tiles and strange uneven shapes, and you're halfway there. The bar is chipped and the tables and chairs are closer to flea market than to Philippe Starck. If you're beginning to tire of overpriced espresso in fussy interiors, head over to the boulevard du Port Royal and relax in 1950s anti-chic.

There are some places in the French capital that don't seem in the least Parisian. One of them is the Banal. Tasteless, tacky, and cheap—that's the look at this student watering-hole on

the long dreary boulevard Port-Royal, south of the Sorbonne. None of this undermines its strong attraction to the student set, who come here in great numbers.

The not-so-secret appeal is that everything here is very cheap, and you're surrounded by crowds of people enjoying themselves. Beer is inexpensive, currently 1.50 euros, and a heaping plate of *frites* the same price. The burly waiter may look like a larger version of the late Egyptian strongman, Gamal Abdul Nasser, but he's friendly and even funny. We were barely into our second beer and had hardly touched the mountain of hot crisp French fries when we'd decided in favor of the Banal.

The Banal succeeds despite the smoke, the noise, and the erratic decor. But there's a lot to like: the friendly staff, the lively music, the young people having fun, the irreverent signs like "Beer—Helping Ugly People Have Sex since 1862."

Here you'll see many frenetic students, some professorial types, a few regulars from the neighborhood: the young scene in action. There are mature heads about, usually hiding in left-wing journals, but almost everybody else is in their early twenties and they're all talking at once. Many of them smoke. Some, upon leaving, don motorcycle helmets. "Nobody Loves You When You're Down and Out," was playing as we entered—although we suspect that they might at the Banal.

## Café Charbon

**109 rue Oberkampf, 75011 (01.43.57.55.13); Métro: Parmentier**
**Open daily, Mon–Fri 9AM–2AM, Sat–Sun 9AM–4AM**

Like other large cities, Paris is a place of fads and fashions, of places that mysteriously become "in" and then, just as quickly, fall "out." A hitherto obscure part of the city is periodically being rediscovered by the young and trendy set, a neighborhood that for a time is considered new and exciting. There are, for instance, a number of recent cafés that one could call dens of "instant antiquity," skillfully designed to look old, located on the rue Oberkampf, a poor and ethnically mixed area.

The Café Charbon was the first of these fashionable and widely talked-about cafés. But unlike some of its neighbors, the Charbon actually is old. Back in the 1880s it was a café-theater. Later it became a *bar-tabac*, selling drinks, cigarettes, and *pari-mutuel* betting tickets. In 1996, Olivier, the present owner, found that the place had real potential, so he took a chance and invested in it. Much restoration was needed, and he had it done with taste and restraint.

Most Parisian cafés are rather quiet places; in public the French speak in hushed, almost conspiratorial tones. But not here. These are younger people chatting with their friends, and at least for the few minutes that they're here, they've discarded the traditional French public image.

The Café Charbon looks as if it has been sitting here dispensing coffee for hundreds of years, all the while sinking into a kind of artistic decadence. Here is a sense of the Belle Epoque, with the lofty ceilings, mirrors, and murals all moodily lit. It's a room of dark shadows, old wood, and fading mirrors. In warm weather, the large doors in front are flung open and light pours into the café.

The bar is usually crowded, but almost by magic, one or two places will usually open up for you. Overhead are strange lighting fixtures that suggest the eyes of great prehistoric insects, peering into your soul. The banquettes behind us were filling up with young people; in front of us were the old bar cupboards with their heavy fittings. After a brief struggle with a blender, the barman was successful, triumphantly bearing off a banana shake. Perhaps it would go to the girl at the back.

Two young Parisiennes with long straight hair were sipping white Burgundy from appropriate glasses. Beside them, elegant young men in jeans and expensive shirts whispered something, and then everyone laughed. You suspect that each person here could have a story to tell. For a few moments this dark place might seem rather sinister, but the Charbon is not unfriendly.

Following on the success of the Charbon, the rue Oberkampf has become a hot spot for trendy boutiques as well as other newer cafés. A café can be more than just a place to eat or drink; it can be the catalyst for changing a neighborhood.

## La Fourmi

**74 rue des Martyrs, 75018 (01.42.64.70.35); Métro: Pigalle. Open daily: Mon–Sat 8AM–2AM, Sun 10AM–2AM**

La Fourmi is in Pigalle, a part of Paris where one might not normally go. In *Rendezvous Eighteenth*, Jake Lamar depicts the Pigalle neighborhood as "the neon-bathed commercial sleaze district, boasting round-the-clock peep shows, leather underwear shops and the International Erotic Museum…" Nevertheless, this area is currently "hot." Celebrities, actors, and designers including Jean-Paul Gaultier, Claude Lelouch, and Johnny Depp have been buying into this area.

Inside La Fourmi, not much has changed in recent years except that it's funkier and artsier than ever, and filled with *gauchistes* and artists with stringy hair. It's a long narrow room where you can browse the stack of multicolored notices and free postcards to find out what's on, what's in, what must be seen, what's chic, and what's free.

La Fourmi appears to have been put together using unsold items from an auction, but the interior was probably carefully designed. The floor has many broken tiles, the background music is New Age cool. The walls are the usual sponged ochre, the tables old oak: elaborate shelves behind the bar seem to be built out of boxes. Cigarette butts and sugar wrappers are allowed to collect on the floor during the day. A copy of the left-wing newspaper *Libération*, with its distinctive red-and-black logo, is usually left around.

Outside is the normal grunge of the boulevard de Rochechouart, with its sex-shops, strange nightclubs, and seedy bars. La Fourmi is an island, and, except for the thumping music overhead, you might almost expect a poet to be ensconced in the corner on a Thonet chair, scribbling his verses.

This is a place for intensely wound-up young people, although we noticed that the front table was taken up by two elderly men playing chess on an antique board. We wondered what they thought of the young man wearing something we'd never seen there before: ankle cuffs with spikes protruding outwards.

La Fourmi's symbol, a stylized ant, is cut into an iron plaque at the bar. "Work—produce something—enjoy" could be the slogan here. It looks like a creative crowd.

# Chez Gladines

**30 rue des Cinq-Diamants, 75013 (01.45.80.70.10); Métro: Corvisart. Open daily noon–3AM, 7PM–midnight; Closed August.**

It's a slice of old Paris, a corner bistro dating from the early twentieth century and well off the tourist circuit. A half-hearted attempt was made to modernize Chez Gladines in the 1930s and then it was left essentially unchanged. We found the entrance to this café almost blocked by young people when we went there last. Soon, though, we were seated at one of the long tables covered with red-and-white checked oilcloth, elbow-to-elbow with students. Many of them were wolfing down immense salads served in dishes of a size more commonly used as mixing bowls. Service was provided by a hardworking girl with a glint in her eye and a diamond in her nose.

A ring of people two or three deep were standing by the 1950s-design bar, under a ceiling in soft yellow with Art Moderne moldings. A Basque influence was evident all around, in the black-and-white photographs, the pelote bat on the wall and the large leather winesack over the door.

When we asked our waitress about the clientele, she said they were mostly from the *fac*—the university—students and professors.

# Café de l'Industrie

**16 rue St. Sabin, 75011**
**(01.47.00.13.53)**
**Métro: Bastille**
**Open daily 10:30AM–2AM**

*I*f Bogart had owned a Paris café before heading off to Casablanca to take over Rick's and meet Ingrid Bergman, this might well have been the one.

The Café de l'Industrie has, if not a North African look, at least a tropical flavor: slow-moving ceiling fans, zebra skin, ferns, African masks, and a clientele that manages to appear artistic, sophisticated, and intellectual, all at the same time.

Years ago when we first went to this café, it was on the edge of a grubby part of Paris and the habitués could have been out-of-work existentialists. Our impression was of a place that seemed faded and outmoded. Now the same interior is up-to-date retro.

The Café de l'Industrie is a fashionable place in what has now become a highly desirable neighborhood, the counterpart of New York's Greenwich Village or London's Chelsea. It's not just popular with students: people from the area stop at this café after shopping, in the course of a walk, or on the way to somewhere else, as did the gray-haired *intello* reading at the bar. Many of the poor and artistic people who originally made this area special have moved out to other parts of the city.

In the first room the salmon-pink, black, and blue-gray bar is tended by a slender young Asian woman with discreet tattoos and a pierced lip. Clad in close-fitting leather, she pours drinks with impressive speed. Next we notice the mysterious corkscrew cast-iron staircase winding up to the next floor, looking like a design from a Victorian etching. (We've never actually seen anyone using the stairs.) The dining rooms are packed—a muffled chatter emerges from the people happily lunching inside.

Low-priced lunches, amiable young servers, a funky, fun interior, a variety of food and wine choices, a location near the Bastille and not far from the Marais—these all help to explain l'Industrie's popularity. So does the excellent coffee, stylishly served in a glass cup with a metal frame and saucer, like something from a museum shop.

And then there's the wildly original decor. We see a profusion of prints, paintings, posters, and a collection of unrelated objects. Large framed oils, huge potted plants, an *ardoise* lettered with food and drink choices—no limit to the creativity here. There's so much to see that we barely notice the large rhino head mounted over the kitchen doorway.

Another time we arrive in the middle of an afternoon, too late for lunch, too early for a pre-dinner drink. The Café de l'Industrie is still lively. People come here to work on projects, equipped with laptops and with documents stuffed into folders. The café is spacious—there's room to spread out one's materials and do creative work. For people living in the typically space-cramped Parisian apartments, that alone would be enough.

"This café has a good feeling about it," remarked a friend after we had sat there for a while.

We agree.

# Le Panier

**32 Place Sainte-Marthe, 75010 (01.42.01.38.18); Métro: Belleville. Open Tues–Sun 11AM–2AM**

The last time we approached this square was at night: as we noted in our book *Paris by Bistro*, in this *quartier* the dogs are not pedigreed and a parked car may lack a hubcap. Darkness is kind to the Place Sainte-Marthe. It hides the dingy stained concrete of the buildings on the square, the turquoise paint flaking off the *Cordonnerie* across the way, the gray satellite dish perched precariously on a tiny first-floor balcony next to laundry flapping in the wind. A bit of gloom can be useful—it obscures the only prosperous-looking building on the square besides the cafés, the mission for the *Sans-Logis* or homeless.

But cafés now dominate the square: the Panier, the Galopin, the Ste. Marthe, and the Panier, flaunting their own awnings in dark red, shamrock green, and scarlet, respectively. To this Le Panier adds a surprising touch of orange and indigo, creating a happy and erratic mix of colors to match the music emanating from within. The flamboyant tones of the Panier are no surprise. The owner, Olivier Colombe, although Parisian by birth, took his inspiration from a quarter in Marseille and came back to create this place on his own, doing the work himself and applying the hot colors of the South. Inside, the burnt oranges and deep crimsons are set off by a sea-green ceiling.

There's a young clientele wearing T-shirts and jeans in warm weather, and jackets on cool evenings. We noticed one young Parisienne in a leather jacket with a silk scarf tied oh-so-elegantly. Here the waiters don't wear tuxedos or even white shirts. They're more likely to don T-shirts, jeans—the same uniform as the customers—and put on cheap athletic shoes from the flea market before they come in to work.

Young people like Le Panier and the other cafés on the square. They come for the wide and uncrowded *terrasse*, the casual and relaxed ambience, the feeling of escape from the city. Except for the accents around you, you could well imagine yourself sampling local cheeses and wines in some small restaurant in the country. European tourists are starting to come here too, attracted by the serious food and decent wine list: A table of older people near us were speaking Dutch. Like most cafés, the Panier has hours when it becomes more of a restaurant, and these are the times that pay its bills. Still, come for a drink and experience "little Marseille." You'll leave with a better sense of the variety to be found in this extraordinary city.

## Lou Pascalou

**14 rue des Panoyaux, 75020 (01.46.36.78.10); Métro: Ménilmontant or Père Lachaise. Open daily 9:30AM–2AM**

In recent years, people have been rediscovering the Paris of Edith Piaf, the hitherto unfashionable 20th arrondissement.

Nothing embodies the trend quite as much as the café Lou Pascalou, at the end of the boulevard Ménilmontant, a large and untidy street lined with Asian, North African, and other restaurants. Ordinary people live here. Dogs bark and children cry. Old ladies lug their packages out of the Arab grocery on the corner. People stop and greet each other on the street, punctuating their greetings with much French handshaking. The quarter is vibrant with life even late in the evenings.

Lou Pascalou fits in perfectly. Its vivid colors shout Provence and the Mediterranean. With young people coming in from all over Paris, Lou Pascalou is usually bursting with activity. Actors and film industry people come here, as do young professionals with their computers and people simply wanting a break from routine. More than a few of them are choosing to settle down and live in this area.

# Chez Prune

**36 rue Beaurepaire, 75010 (01.42.41.30.47); Métro: Jacques Bonsergent.**
**Open daily 9AM–2AM**

Located on the Canal St. Martin, not far from the Hôtel du Nord made famous by the film of the same name, Chez Prune has succeeded in creating a large and enthusiastic following among the young. This café is in a part of Paris that used to be considered drab and even somewhat questionable, but in recent years it has turned into one of the up-and-coming neighborhoods, with prices of apartments near the canal rising rapidly. The trend wasn't hurt by the use of the Canal St. Martin, with its picturesque iron bridges, as one of the settings in the film *Amélie*.

Chez Prune is usually bursting at the seams, especially at night, and on Friday and Saturday nights people line up on the sidewalk for an evening of live music.

With its rich, lively colors and shabby chic "look," Chez Prune might have been decorated by the same people who wait tables there. It's animated, it's fun, and it draws an urbane crowd. A short distance from La Patache (see Chapter V: A Nineteenth-Century Look), Chez Prune is worlds away in spirit.

## · 7 ·

## CAFÉS PLUS

*Music is your own experience, your own thoughts, your wisdom.
If you don't live it, it won't come out of your horn.*
—Charlie Parker

*T*here are some cafés that defy the narrow definitions and go beyond what a café is normally expected to be. Although the Paris café scene doesn't offer the range of entertainment that London pubs had in the old days—besides the usual dart games, we recall that some pubs even offered striptease—the café can have more for you than just food, drink, and conversation.

It's clear that Parisians take both their cafés and their intellectuals seriously. (Paris is a city where streets have been named for great writers, not to mention British kings and American presidents.) Starting in 1992 with Le Café des Phares at the Bastille, specialized cafés that provided organized philosophical discussion started to spring up all over Paris.

And as computer use has grown widespread, cybercafés have become scattered throughout the city, although they are not as common as they once were now that inexpensive broadband connection is available to anyone with a telephone connection. (McDonald's, that archrival of the Paris café, lures customers by providing free wireless Internet connections.)

There are other cafés where writers gather to discuss their work. Some cafés even offer theatrical evenings; others have sessions in which psychological issues can be discussed; and in at least one café, people can receive psychotherapy, for a fee, of course.

A few cafés regularly schedule music, usually jazz. Others offer presentations of folk music or rock. The accordion player and the middle-aged woman singing nostalgic songs in the manner of Edith Piaf—a very French combination of sentimentality and cynicism—these symbols of Paris to so many fans of old movies are actually becoming hard to find.

Perhaps you've been in Paris for a few days, and you find yourself craving a little excitement, some nightlife. A café offering entertainment might be just what you want.

There's a growing trend to provide live music on weekends at least, and sometimes during the week. Often the musicians are young and the entrance fee is the price of a drink. Other cafés may have a small cover charge, depending on the price of the talent they've recruited.

# Haynes

**3 rue Clauzel, 75009 (01.48.78.40.63)**
**Métro: St. Georges**
**Open Tues–Sun 7PM–midnight**
**Cover charge (on music nights) 5 euros**
**Music Thurs–Sun evenings**

*D*on't be put off by the old sign outside, its cracked plastic announcing a "Restaurant American." At Haynes you can have a drink, taste an hors d'oeuvre, and for a small entrance fee on the nights when there's entertainment—generally Thursday through Saturday—listen to good music. On Sunday nights lately there's been dancing to the music of Brazil.

Haynes has been "cooking" in both a musical and a culinary way for about 50 years now, and it's become something of an historic landmark. Haynes is an original, a Paris institution. It was founded by Leroy Haynes, an African-American G.I. who decided to stay on after WWII and prepare

classic Southern food for homesick black soldiers. Later he founded this restaurant at 9 rue Clauzel.

"G.I.'s made Haynes's famous," recalled Don Corinaldi, a former cook there. "The word spread and… famous artists like Billie Holiday, Count Basie, Louis Armstrong, and Duke Ellington were coming in regularly… They recommended Haynes to their friends, other musicians and celebrities like Harry Belafonte, Richard Burton, and Elizabeth Taylor. Today most of our clientele is French."

Since Leroy's death, Haynes has been kept up by his widow, Maria. You can find it on the end of a dark and obscure street in an unfashionable district, exuding warmth and hospitality and providing good jazz several nights a week. A little less famous than it once was—you might not have difficulty finding a table these days—Haynes deserves wider recognition.

Over the years it seems that almost everybody has found their way here. On our last visit, we sat under a large and personally autographed photo of Elizabeth Taylor and Richard Burton, and looked at framed pictures of other "greats" who've stopped by, people like

Miles Davis, Dizzy Gillespie, Sidney Poitier, Ray Charles, and Marianne Faithful, to mention a few.

One of the framed photos belongs to another Haynes institution: look carefully and you'll see a black-and-white photo of the maitre d', Benny Luke, from the days when he played the role of Jakob, first on stage and then in the film *Cage aux Folles*. Getting to meet him is reason enough for making a stop at Haynes. An expatriate American himself, Benny originally studied dance on the G.I. Bill (he was evidently more successful in this than Art Buchwald, another veteran, was in his efforts to learn French) and came to Paris to find work. And find it he did. Dancing at the Folies Bergère, acting with the *Cage Aux Folles* company for years on stage and later on screen—this is how Benny, like many other Americans, made his mark on the culture he chose to live in. Now he's become part of the action at Haynes again, moving gracefully about, greeting newcomers, showing them to tables, pouring drinks, making everyone feel at ease. He's witty, he's charming, and he's good at what he does.

Any café and musical venue that's fifty years old will have had its ups and downs, and Haynes is no exception. A few years ago it had the forlorn appearance of a run-down rural Missouri roadhouse, but now it looks good again. The interior has been redone and is brighter and more inviting. The talented new cook, a woman from Chicago, learned her craft in Paris at the Cordon Bleu. We're sure that LeRoy Haynes wouldn't have known what to think of that.

# La Chope des Puces

**122 rue des Rosiers, 93400 St. Ouen (01.40.11.02.49); Métro: Clignancourt.
Open 8AM–9PM Sat, Sun, and holidays. Music 2–7PM**

It's a small, drab hole-in-the-wall off the rue des Rosiers in the north part of the massive flea market that begins at Clignancourt. The decor is dismal, plain and frumpy—but oh, that jazz!

We drifted in on a chilly afternoon in April, attracted by the description given to us by Aline, an antique dealer whose shop at the nearby Paul Bert market deals in high-quality vintage food and wine-related items.

On Saturday afternoons the Chope des Puces is packed with people. Many are antique dealers, but some are other Paris residents and tourists. In *Paris to the Moon*, Adam Gopnik, who writes for the *New Yorker*, recalled a visit with his small son Luke:

> After lunch, on this freezing, cold day, faint light raking through the stalls, Luke and I stop at the little bar with a Django-style swing band, two gypsy guitarists with ancient electrics with f-holes, joined by a good-looking blonde with an alto sax… They played the old American songs—"All of Me," "There Will Never Be Another You"—some Jobim too, really swinging it… A perfect half hour.

The prices listed outside for each *consommation* go up 2 or 3 euros when there's live music, as there was on this Saturday—but no one was complaining. Everybody was taken with the inspired jazz guitar from Mondine Garcia and his son Ninine, two Gypsies (or Romanies) who play in the tradition of Django Rheinhart. Passersby stopped and peered in to see if there was room inside to crowd yet another listener in to hear the spirited, joyous performance. A petite, trench-coated French woman joined in, supplying words in convincing English—her variations on the theme of "Summertime" suggesting to us that she, too, might be a professional musician.

At the Chope des Puces, the floor tiles are patterns straight out of Escher; the bar is chipped New Jersey diner, and the lights are cheap and flickering fluorescent. Formica is favored and old is everywhere. The walls are thick with black-and-white photos of musicians, most of them old-fashioned-looking locals. There are only two small low tables and two even smaller high tables, but you'll be lucky if any are free. Almost everybody stands at the bar and mingles with the musicians.

The last time we were there, two young women, possibly French film students, were photographing the musicians and probably us as well. It was clear that they recognized the authenticity and charm of this place. Go on the weekends, between 2:00 and 7:00PM. You won't be sorry.

(If you're into antiques and collectibles, you might also want to look up the Village Suisse antique market in the 15th arrondissement, mentioned in Chapter VIII: Tourists' Cafés. And of course you'll want to visit the famed Hôtel Drouot auction house.)

## Le Bistro des Vosges

**31 blvd Beaumarchais, 75004 (01.42.72.94.85); Métro: Bastille. Open daily 7AM–midnight**

Although we didn't have time to visit the Bistro des Vosges, we include it in our list because of its central location near the Bastille and the Marais, and because this café currently offers live music five nights a week. As the owner explained to us, from

Sunday to Wednesday there's piano bar from 7:30 to 10:30PM, and on Thursdays there's a jazz ensemble from 8:00 to 10:30PM.

## Cafés Philo

There are a number of cafés, in addition to the well-known Café des Phares at the Bastille, which from time to time have organized discussions of philosophy. In France philosophy is a required course for most ambitious high school students, and the annual questions for the philosophy part of the baccalaureate or "bac," the series of grueling high school exit examinations that students have to pass to go on to university, are debated later on in a thousand cafés throughout the country. We recall that one year the question asked of 18-year-olds was "When did time begin?" Some cafés in Paris have organized discussion sessions led by philosophy professors with the patrons joining in. The Café de Flore (see Chapter II: Legends of Literature and Art) has had philosophical sessions in English. The French event magazines such as *Pariscope* or the English *Time Out* might be the best source of current information about what's on and where.

# Café Universel

**267 rue St. Jacques, 75005**
**(01.43.25.74.20)**
**RER: Luxembourg**
**Open Mon–Sat 9:30AM–2:00AM**
**Live music from 9:30PM**
**No admission charge**

You know that the Universel is serious about music when you step in and see a shiny new Yamaha grand piano onstage, well tuned and flooded in halogen light.

Be warned: if you wish to escape from the strong American influence lapping at the edges of the Parisian youth culture, you might want to avoid this old-fashioned café south of the university area. If you do come here, you'll be greeted outside by a dignified cigar-store Indian, and, immediately inside to your right, by a Statue of Liberty holding a neon flame of red, white, and blue. American license plates from the North to the South, and from Massachusetts to Utah—the full political spectrum—are tacked up on walls and ceilings. Stone walls and beamed ceilings with stars suggest the image of an American flag. Signs in paper and neon, old phonograph records, and bottles of various spirits are crammed together behind the bar, suggesting that all this was an unplanned and spontaneous growth.

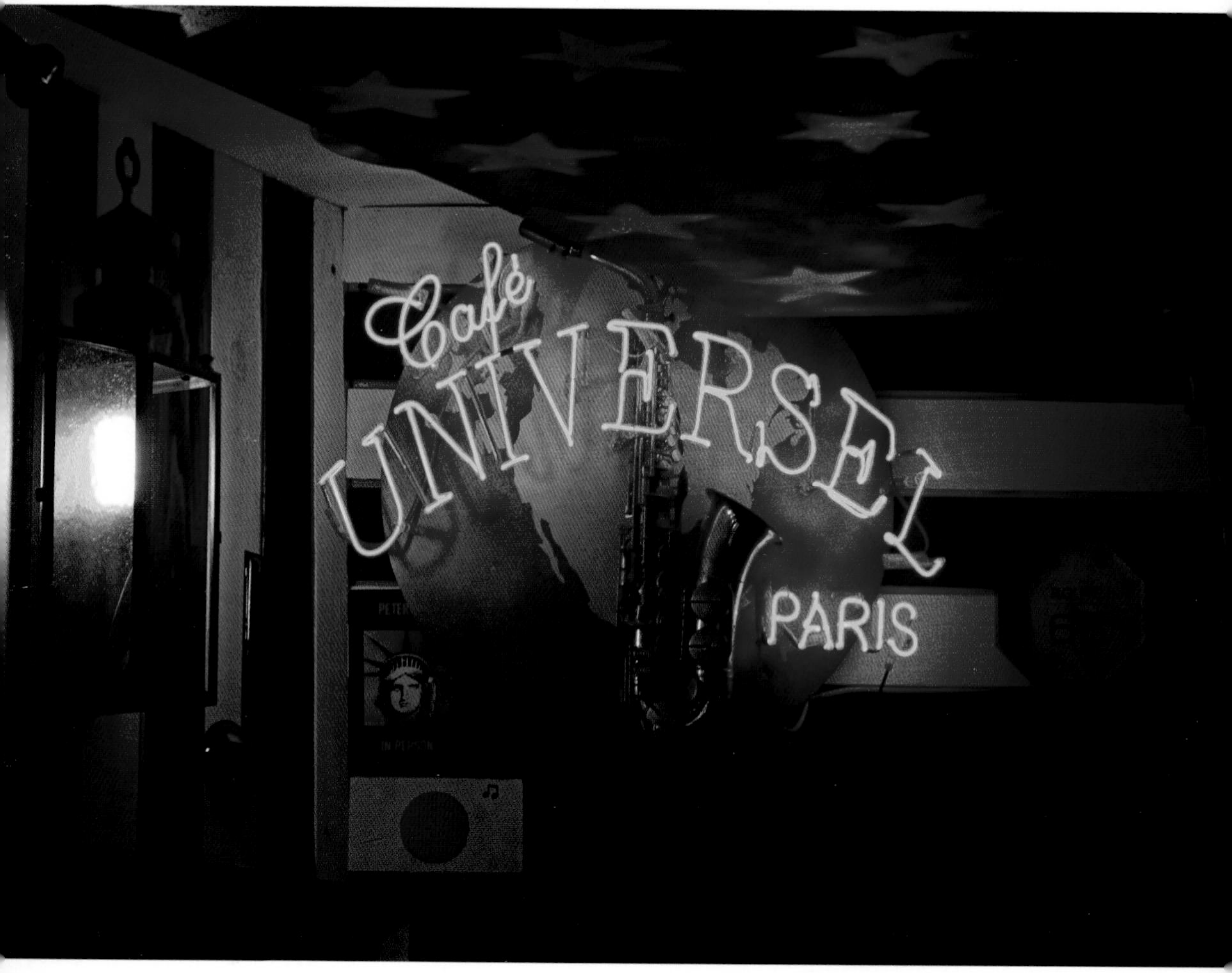
Café
UNIVERSEL
PARIS

This building is old, even for Paris, dating from well before the French Revolution, and the oldest part of the Café Universel seems almost carved out of rock. The darkness is punctuated by small neon signs, tiny spotlights, and a large, dramatic red sign, "Café Universel," lights up the area where the musicians will appear.

Here Fazia and Abou Kemel run a warm intimate café that turns into a jazz club in the evenings. Music is on almost every night and it's not expensive. The jazz is mainstream, mostly from the Golden Age of the '50s and '60s, although Brazilian jazz is sometimes featured.

We wandered into the Café Universel on a week night and heard a charming and sensuous young singer, Deborah Benassouli, singing the old standards accompanied by a trio. Like most of the musicians appearing at the Universel, she's just launching her musical career. That night her listeners were mostly French people from the neighborhood, but the Café Universel has drawn notables in the audience in the past, including the late Miles Davis. Other celebrities drop in from time to time, as well as politicians, business people, and tourists.

An appealing café during the daytime, the Universel is a must in the evenings. It's retro, it's fun, it's funky, and friendly. It brings to mind the jazz clubs and musicians of a different era. And at the Universel, the best seats are set aside for non-smokers. When we left, Billie Holiday was singing softly out of somewhere.

· 8 ·

# TOURIST CAFÉS

*So much of who we are is where we have been.*
—William Langewiesche

*W*hen you go to Paris for the first time, or even the tenth, you expect to see the famous places. And afterwards you might want to stop for a reviving drink at a nearby café. We all know what the "musts" are: the Eiffel Tower, Notre Dame, the Arc de Triomphe, the Champs-Elysées, the Louvre Museum, and, of course, Montmartre, especially the Place du Tertre with its itinerant artists. The cafés clustered around these attractions are not always the best in Paris, but we have found a few that we like.

A number of cafés, all of them expensive, are near the Trocadero, the area closest to the Eiffel Tower. Only one, the Café Trocadero, has tables with a view of the Eiffel Tower, but in the summer the view is obscured by trees. A better choice for viewing the famous tower from a café table can be found further down the river near the métro Alma Marceau. No particularly memorable cafés are near Notre Dame, although there are certainly some famous restaurants.

The greatest people-watching street in Paris is the Champs-Elysées, the wide, tree-lined boulevard with the Arc de Triomphe at one end and a series of parks and gardens at the other. The Champs-Elysées has a number of outdoor cafés that provide a view of the famous arch. However there's a wide disparity in quality among them: some are ordinary and overpriced and many of the others are noisy fast-food outlets.

So to make your journey through Paris's attractions a little easier, we offer a few of our choices near key monuments. These cafés may not have quite the charm and personality of some of the smaller cafés mentioned elsewhere in this book, but they're well located and generally tourist-friendly. And another advantage: most of them are open all day, every day, and into the night.

## ARC DE TRIOMPHE AND CHAMPS-ELYSÉES

# Le Deauville

**75 ave des Champs-Elysées, 75008
(01.42.25.08.64)
Métro: George V
Open daily, Mon–Fri 7:30AM–3AM,
Sat–Sun 7:30AM–4AM**

*I*f the ebb and flow of the activity on the Champs-Elysées reminds you of a tide, think of the Deauville as an appropriate port. Its theme is nautical, with blue and white the signature colors on the spacious terrace.

A trip to the Normandy coast a few days before put us in just the right mood for Le Deauville. Here a sleek, glossy, interior contrasts with the simpler terrace. The waiters in their Breton sailor jerseys look a little out of place inside the polished luxury of the Deauville, with its dark mirrored ceiling, heavy chrome fittings, teak floor, modern brass bar, and elaborate ship's-lantern lighting. No matter—their smiles are friendly, their service prompt. The interior here makes one think of a first-class *salon* in a luxury liner: the designer chairs are two-toned, cherry and taupe, beside small cherry tables. The signature horseracing motif suggests the pleasures of the real Deauville. This motif is repeated on the burgundy-and-white menus and in frosted

glass on the great mirrored wall at the back. And for sports fans, a discreetly placed wide-screen TV broadcasts the latest sporting event.

Elegant Parisians of all ages, smartly-dressed business people clutching cell phones, youngsters teetering along on skateboards, a couple pushing a stroller, numer-ous tourists: a lively parade streams by. The patrons of Le Deauville are travelers from everywhere, and since this is one of the less expensive cafés in the area, it also attracts a fair number of people who live or work nearby. We sat next to a well-dressed German reading *Die Welt*. We heard Italian spoken behind us, and unrecognized languages from Asia and Africa further back.

The menu has the kind of graphic design one ought to frame, and we're sure some people have. It's burgundy and white, Art Deco in style, with the silhouettes of a sleek racehorse and jockey accompanied by a lean and graceful Russian dog, the Borzoi. The city of Deauville is famous for its racetrack, casino, yacht-filled harbor, and beautiful but reportedly superficial people. (The small public library there closed down some time ago and no one seemed to notice.) The Borzoi, stylish though supposedly lacking in intelligence, might be a perfect symbol.

Le Deauville is elegant, friendly, and perfectly located for people-watching on the Champs-Elysées. Sitting at a table in front of the Deauville, you have the feeling that the world will eventually pass by. Someone at the same table 50 years ago might have seen Fred Astaire dancing down the street for the filming of *Funny Face*.

EIFFEL TOWER

# Chez Francis

**7 Place de l'Alma, 75008**
**(01.47.20.86.83)**
**Métro: Alma-Marceau**
**Open daily noon–1AM**

*P*aris has two major avenues of special extravagance and obvious wealth. One is the avenue George V. If you ever see a yellow Ferrari, a silver Bentley, and the long black Mercedes of a rock star lined up together, it will be here. The flagship store of Louis Vuitton is at one end of the avenue; the Crazy Horse, the world's most famous strip club, is at the other.

The other legendary street of unbridled hedonism is the avenue Montaigne, where many of the great fashion houses maintain boutiques. Where the avenues George V and Montaigne meet is Chez Francis. A superb setting for observing the "beautiful people," the terrace offers a clear view of the Eiffel Tower as well as the Seine and Left Bank. (It's also near the spot where Princess Diana was in her tragic accident.)

Polished, plush, and polite is Chez Francis, with velvet banquettes, quiet and courteous greetings, and the rich fragrance of Cuban cigars. The shiny black bar, the fringed lamps shaded in pink and russet and the coral marble floor suggest the best of Las Vegas. Over the bar is a display of a range of drinks with numerous whiskeys including unusual single malts. The second room, seen from the bar, is brightened with azaleas and lined with a semicircle of mirrors. Here you feel cosseted, catered to, comforted.

This is now more of a restaurant than a café, with its heavy white tablecloths—but avoid the classic French dining hours and you can sit at a terrace table with a view of the real attraction, the Eiffel Tower. From the terrace you can see the river, the *bateaux mouches*, and the famous tower. (At peak hours you may wish to sit inside at the bar if all you want is a drink.)

Arthur Power, a writer for the *New York Herald*, recalled stopping here with James Joyce:

> This café was a favourite haunt of Joyce's at this time, and here he would drink a Cinzano à l'eau, its rich ruby color being more evocative than its alcoholic content, and discuss Irish literature, Dublin, and the disadvantages of possessing a Celtic temperament. After a while we would return to the flat where Mrs. Joyce would provide an excellent dinner…

These days Chez Francis brings in businessmen at lunch, and people from the quartier as well as tourists in the evenings. It's not cheap, with coffee starting at 3.50 euros, but James Joyce never looked at prices, and sometimes you shouldn't either.

Suddenly the hush is broken by a dozen or so Irish revelers, just come in from the cold. A generous Irish hotelkeeper has given his staff a mid-week break, a trip to Paris. They entertain us with their stories of Ireland, of the celebrating they've done and plan to do, of how much they love this city.

Chez Francis could be an ideal spot to begin your Paris adventure.

# Le Café du Marché

**38 rue Cler, 75007**
**(01.47.05.51.27)**
**Métro: École Militaire**
**Open daily Mon–Sat 7AM–midnight, Sun to 4:30PM**

*F*or many knowledgeable Parisians, and also for large numbers of well-off foreigners, the 7th is the arrondissement of choice. The seat of government is here, and many of the top people in journalism and entertainment have chosen to settle in this area. Cole Porter lived in the 7th; so does the Prime Minister of France. Rodin's studio, now a museum, is in this *quartier* on the rue de Varenne. The very symbol of Paris, the Eiffel Tower, is in this district. The 7th is an area of old money, privacy, and aristocracy, of what people call "high walls and heavy doors."

The Café du Marché is a well-liked stop on a pedestrian street near Les Invalides. You'll hear a lot of English and a variety of foreign languages on this pleasantly large terrace. Tourists have discovered this café and why not? It's not too far from Eiffel's tower and close to Napoleon's tomb. In the off-season, you'll see mostly French people taking advantage of the café's good location and reasonable prices; it's a great spot for studying the street life, a cafégoer's delight.

LE MUSÉE DU LOUVRE

## *Le Fumoir*

**6 rue de l'Amiral Coligny, 75001
(01.42.92.00.24); Métro: Louvre-Rivoli.
Open daily 11AM–2AM**

Sleek, slick, sensual, and oh, so nice is Le Fumoir. Here is your reward for the long slog down the marble halls of the Louvre. Here are pillars done in shiny *café au lait*, subtle concealed lighting, a *nouvelle* version of a Deco mural on one wall, rich wood floors, and long almond drapes against the milk-chocolate walls. In the background you hear familiar music from the 1920s and '30s, much of it by George Gershwin and Cole Porter. Le Fumoir is well situated. To the north, you see the Louvre, which glows incandescent at dusk. To the west, you have a view of the Seine, and across the river, the Left Bank.

And it pulls them in—the young professionals, the *branchés*, the style setters. Highly attractive young people crowd around, but there's every incentive not to look at them, but to pick up a newspaper or magazine instead; even in English the selection here is impressive. Would you like to read the *Times Literary Supplement*, the *Nation,* the *Independent?* They're all here, and in the latest edition. So are periodicals in French, German, and even Japanese. The only drawback on a cloudy day is the low light—one squints at the fine print. If you head for the back room you'll find

yourself in what looks like an immense library with shelves stuffed with books. But many of the patrons, we suspect, might be more interested in the vagaries of design than in the intellectual fashions of the day.

Our small cups of espresso come with a little dish of thin gingersnaps, an intriguing alternative to chocolate. We sip the coffee, noticing the foot traffic past this end of the Louvre, enjoying the serenity of the late afternoon. Writers could do their work here—we see several people with paper or laptops. One of the newer cafés, Le Fumoir succeeds admirably. We could easily be tempted to become regulars.

NOTRE DAME AND LA SAINTE CHAPELLE

# Bar du Caveau

**17 Place Dauphine, 75006; (01.43.54.45.95); Métro: Cité. Open Mon–Sat 8:30AM–6:30PM May–Sept; Open Mon–Fri Oct–April**

The Place Dauphine is a secret garden hidden away behind the Conciergerie. Many Parisians don't know about it. The beauty of this quiet hideaway, tucked into the Place behind the Conciergerie—and a convenient stop if you're going to or coming from a visit to la Sainte Chapelle—makes up for the rather austere behavior of the people behind the bar.

The old mural along one wall gives you a sense of what life beside the Seine might have looked like long ago. While you're there sipping a drink, you may want to peruse the daily newspapers or the glossy magazines that are available, their articles relating to country living, high-priced sports cars, and the good life.

MARAIS AND PLACE DES VOSGES

# Ma Bourgogne

**19 Place des Vosges, 75004**
**(01.42.78.44.64)**
**Métro: Bastille**
**Open daily 8AM–1:30AM. No credit cards**

*E*ven in Paris it's hard to imagine a more romantic setting for a café than that of Ma Bourgogne, a very old café that in an earlier incarnation as a *tabac* was used in Georges Simenon's *Maigret* mysteries. The Place des Vosges is no ordinary neighborhood, and the regulars at this café include French politicians and people from the world of television and film. A number of names were dropped during a brief conversation with a waiter, a few of which would be familiar even to people outside France.

The Place des Vosges was one of the world's first planned communities. Constructed in the early 1600s by the King of France for the nobility, it's a square city block of magnificent townhouses with steep roofs and romantic dormers, all surrounding a small park. There's a pleasing regularity to the vaulted ceilings, the red

brick contrasting with the white. In the old days when it was called the Place Royale, noblemen would sometimes settle their disputes by fighting duels in this square. The cover of Ma Bourgogne's wine list gives the cafégoer a few details about this famous square, the addresses of the pavilions of the King and Queen, Madame de Sévigné's birthplace, and Victor Hugo's home.

The terrace is deservedly popular. We arrived there on a cold, misty night in late November and soon found ourselves warm under the large gas-fired heaters, sipping Ma Bourgogne's excellent *café allongé*, a big cup just the thing for a chilly day. From the terrace we could see the great arches of the Place des Vosges and the walkways that extend around all four sides of the park.

On another visit we sat inside at one of the sturdy tables, a table handcrafted from massive pieces of solid blond oak. It was only about 6:00PM, teatime for many of the French around us. Some tourists from Greece came in when it

was much too early by French standards to expect food. They were given menus, and the waiter did his best to explain the possibilities, using a mixture of French and English.

In the peak periods, stopping for a coffee or a beer would be tolerated only at the bar, but during the afternoons and early evenings you'll see many people holding earnest discussions and indulging in serious flirtation over a drink. Mornings bring out quite a different crowd, and it's a good place to go for your breakfast coffee and croissant. No credit cards: somehow this policy fits in with the mood here.

Amber lights inside cast dark shadows and the mirrors intensify their effect. We noticed the expected red banquettes and the tables covered with pink tablecloths. The large oak cabinets could be antiques from a country inn. There are cafés which come into their own at night: Ma Bourgogne is one of those places.

## RUE MOUFFETARD AND THE OPEN AIR MARKET

*T*here are many roving markets in Paris: we like the Bastille on Thursdays and Sundays, Barbès-Rochechouart on Wednesdays and Saturdays. Friends go to the Tuesday market on boulevard Richard-Lenoir, or the Marché d'Aligre on the street of that name. But there's a most attractive market where the open air stalls are out every day, and that is on the rue Mouffetard, where one has existed for hundreds of years. The variety of fresh fruit, vegetables, breads, cheeses, and many other good things is impressive, and the merchants along this street arrange them with artistic skill.

In *Le Ventre de Paris*, Emile Zola gives us a picture of the tempting produce at an early morning market: "All that was visible in the intermittent light cast by swinging lanterns were the fleshy flowers of a bunch of artichokes, the delicate greens of salads, the pink coral of the carrots."

# Le Verre à Pied

**118 bis, rue Mouffetard 75005 (01.43.31.15.72); Métro: Censier-Daubenton.
Open Tues–Sat 8AM–8PM, Sunday until 3PM. Closed one week in August.**

Most Parisians will seldom, if ever, visit the great historic cafés of literary fame, or go inside the fashionable designer cafés. They're much more likely to hang out at a neighborhood favorite, something like Le Verre à Pied.

The area behind the Sorbonne has been home to countless generations of students. It's an older section of the city and the buildings here are not as high or as elegant as they are further to the west. Years ago this neighborhood was disreputable and rather dangerous, a seedy sort of place. To give an example: after seeing the *clochard* or wino commonly called the "Ratman" in action and telling about him in *The Cafés of Paris*, we lost track of him for several years. An old Paris hand advised us to check the Place de la Contrescarpe, at the north end of the rue Mouffetard, where the *clochards* used to gather.

That has all changed, and now the rue Mouffetard has become of interest to the tourist. Shops here are less expensive than in many other parts of Paris; restaurants are simpler, and there's a small-town feeling about the area.

Le Verre à Pied is a *café-tabac* where tobacco products are sold. (You can also buy métro tickets, telephone cards and stamps there—a *tabac* is handy to have in your neighborhood.) By the door there's a glass cabinet with some thirty types of pipe tobacco. It's a casual place: people fall into conversations with strangers. Le Verre à Pied is very much involved in life on the rue Mouffetard, and the management has a friendly and encouraging attitude towards local artists. The proprietor was helping a young photographer to hang her works on the walls when we arrived.

This café seems to have gone through many generations of owners with differing ideas of design. In some ways, it looks as if the original builders might have had ambitious plans: there's a massive nineteenth-century marble bar that would not be out of place in a major hotel. The molding around the dark cream ceiling is also elaborate, but was probably installed some time later. The fluorescent lights and mismatched tile floor seem out of place, but strangely enough, the whole thing hangs together. For heating there's a large, cast-iron stove, once very common but now seldom seen. In contrast to the complicated bar and the molding in the front of the café, the *toilettes* in the back are the simple, old-fashioned variety commonly known as "Turkish." All that's missing in the picture is the large house dog, which would normally be sprawled out asleep in the doorway.

The clientele is local and almost certainly left wing. Several issues of *Libération* were strewn about as well as posters urging political action. The back room is small and no one sits there unless they have to. Most people stand at the bar, enjoying an excellent cup of Lavazza coffee, a glass of beer, or a small glass of wine at a modest price.

MONTMARTRE

# Café des Deux Moulins

**15 rue Lepic, 75018 (01.42.54.90.50); Métro: Abbesses. Open Mon–Sat 7:30am–2pm, Sat 10AM–2AM**

Famous as the café featured in the hit movie *Amélie*, the Deux Moulins is one that visitors to Paris often put high on their list. The original post-war decor has been preserved, with the copper-topped bar, mustard-colored ceiling, neon lights, and lace curtains. You'd be hard put to find any *Amélie*-like charm in the waiters and waitresses, but the ordinary feeling about this neighborhood hangout may be part of its appeal.

*Amélie* is one of the few French films in recent years to have achieved international success. A café was central to the story and the Deux Moulins was probably chosen in part because it seemed typical, even scruffy. Another reason might be technical: this café is unusual in that it has glass doors opening onto the street not only on the front façade, but also on the side. The available light is much brighter than usual, and the open layout made it easier for the camera people to shoot the scenes.

A few years ago this café was called the Tabac des Deux Moulins, and a writer in Paris's *Free Voice* described it as being "between the tourist hordes of Sacré Coeur and the frantic sleaze of Pigalle," a place where "all types drop in for a quiet, quick drink before doing whatever has to be done that night." (For some reason the "whatever" was not defined.)

# Chez La Mère Catherine

**6 Place du Tertre, 75018 (01.46.06.32.69); Métro: Abbesses. Open daily 11AM–midnight**

Until a hundred or so years ago Montmartre was an independent village to the north of Paris with a raffish and bohemian reputation. Artists lived here and so did some of the poor who worked in Paris. The town square at the top is called the Place du Tertre, and it's famous throughout the world. When people think of artists working on canvases, of windmills perched on the hill, of small houses with shuttered windows clustered along narrow and twisting streets, they're probably imagining Montmartre, possibly as remembered from the works of Utrillo. We all recognize Montmartre in the posters of Toulouse-Lautrec, so familiar now that they've become clichés on shopping bags and tea towels. These images depict riotous living, dancers doing the can-can in decadent cabarets, all of the excesses associated with nightlife in this *quartier* at the turn of the twentieth century.

The best known and oldest café in Montmartre is La Mère Catherine. Founded in 1793 by a real Catherine, Catherine Lemoine, in what was then a small town outside Paris, this café welcomed Danton and other leaders of the Revolution.

Now that those days are over, the Mère Catherine looks like one of the many café-restaurants around the Place du Tertre. But inside you can see that it has clung perversely to a kind of village simplicity, with low ceilings and naïve old oil paintings along the dark walls, a shelf of ceramic jugs, and liquor bottles in no perceptible order. Taken all together, the tables with red-and-white checkered tablecloths, the simple gingham curtains at the windows, the subdued lighting, and the heavy beams black with age—it's what most people would call romantic. This look has been duplicated in "French" cafés from Stockholm to Sacramento. These are the touches one would find at a country inn or in a small town restaurant, which is what Montmartre used to be and still is in some respects. The feeling of being in a nineteenth-century village is what continues to draw crowds of people to the Place du Tertre.

On the walls over the dark framed oils are mottos in French and paintings of the red caps worn by the Jacobins, the rebels during the Revolution. But those are the only signs of revolution here.

At La Mère Catherine, they claim that the use of the word "bistro" (quickly) began in this place, uttered by Cossack troops in 1814 who would stop for an unauthorized drink and use it to demand fast service: they had to get back on duty before their officers found them out.

Less rushed ourselves, we sit in the dark, homey interior and look out at the square. (We're sitting at one of the few tables inside with a view.) It's chilly today and La Mère Catherine warms us, with the friendliness of the server, the low farmhouse ceilings, and the splashes of red here and there. Two pleasant Norwegian women, tourists who have to leave the next day, come in for a glass of wine—it's the same price as coffee. They like this place.

If like most visitors to Paris you go up to Montmartre to see Sacré Coeur, and fight your way through the crowds to the Place du Tertre, you might stop here, at the real, the original café-restaurant on the square. If you sit outside at one of the tables or inside by the window, you'll have a fine view of the Place, with its "artists" sketching portraits of attractive young tourists and the groups of bewildered-looking Europeans and Japanese being led up and down the narrow streets.

BOIS DE VINCENNES

# La Potinière du Lac

**4 Place Edouard Renard 75012 (00.43.43.39.98); Métro: Porte Dorée. Open Tues–Sun from 7AM with early closing 4PM on Tues and 7PM Sun. Otherwise open until 11PM**

Two of our Parisian friends often go for walks in the Bois de Vincennes—they find an hour or so of hiking in the woods very relaxing, almost like a day in the country. Not many tourists make their way out to this park, but for those who do, La Potinière du Lac will be a pleasant stop. If you come here, you'll seat yourself on a large terrace under a broad sweep of burnt orange awning. On the left you'll see a double row of large palm trees—not a common sight in Paris—as well as beds of tropical flowers. In this setting you could quite easily imagine yourself on the French Riviera. It's appropriate that you should see at the end of the street the Musée d'Afrique et d'Océanie, one of the fine but lesser-known Paris museums.

Directly in front of you is the beginning of the vast Bois de Vincennes, with its profusion of verdant plants. There are hundreds of examples of trees, shrubs, and flowers from all over the world. Once the royal hunting grounds for French kings, much of the Bois is still a real forest.

A short distance from your café table is Lake Daumesnil. If you decide not to take a long walk in the Bois, you might consider renting a rowboat and spending a leisurely hour or so on the lake, and, upon your return, stopping for a drink at La Potinière.

### VILLAGE SUISSE ANTIQUE MARKET

*Antique Market open 10:30AM–7PM, every day except Tuesdays and Wednesdays*

## À la Petite Marquise

**50 avenue de la Motte-Picquet, 75015 (01.47.34.94.03); Métro: Motte-Picquet. Open daily 7:30AM–7:45PM, closed Tues**

À La Petite Marquise might not attract much attention by itself. It's a good, fairly typical *salon de thé* near the Village Suisse, or Swiss Village, a collection of specialized high-grade antique shops in the chic part of the 15th, and it's frequented mostly by well-dressed Parisiennes and antique dealers taking a break from work.

You don't go to the Petite Marquise for a view or for glamour; those are things you find elsewhere in the city. (Although we've found that antique dealers tend to know something about food, and can often recommend a good café or an outstanding bistro.)

What the Petite Marquise has going for it is the occasional patronage of an extraordinary dog. The dog is Rostand, named after the French dramatist who wrote *Cyrano de Bergerac*. This Rostand is a Welsh Corgi, the same type of dog favored by the English royal family. He's a Pembrokeshire Corgi, to be specific, a short round little dog remarkable for his large head, short legs, and intense expression. After we'd related a story about the brilliance of our own dog to Ghislaine, the antique store owner, she came back with one that was really worth hearing: her Rostand has taken the Paris métro. By himself.

It happened this way: Ghislaine Chapelier, the proprietress of a rather special little boutique at Village Suisse—she sells antique fans, old jewelry, and a host of charming collectibles—was fully occupied with customers one day. When she looked around for Rostand, a well-behaved animal who normally dozes in his basket in the corner, he wasn't there. She wasn't worried at first—the Village Suisse is a collection of shops where the dealers know each other, and know whose dog belongs to whom. If Rostand had taken it into his mind to take a stroll, she was sure he'd be back before long.

Time passed. She began to get anxious. Then came the telephone call. It was the stationmaster of a far-away métro stop—next to her home, in fact. "I have your dog here," he said, "Do you want me to keep him in my office?" Bored by the antique trade, Rostand had decided to call it a day. He had walked several blocks, gone underground, picked the right train, and jumped off at the correct stop. And a kindly stationmaster made sure that he got home safely.

# CAFÉS BY ARRONDISSEMENT

# INDEX

## A

Antoine, Café, 116

Atelier Renault, 98

Auvergnats, 14–15, 76, 122

## B

Baker, Josephine, 64, 96

Baldwin, James, 10, 36, 42, 55, 57

Banal, Café, 133–134

Bar des Théâtres, 62, **64–65**

Bardot, Brigitte, 109

Beaubourg, Café, 100

Beauvoir, Simone de, 10, 15, 36, 41, 51, 91

Beckett, Samuel, 35

Birkin, Jane, 93

Boubal, Paul, 15

Bougnat, 14

Bourgogne, Ma, 177

Brassaï, 36, 68, 82

Bricolo Café, 102

Buchwald, Art, 20, 64–65, 154

## C

Cafés, *see individual names*

Callaghan, Morley, 37, 39, 47, 48

Camus, Albert, 42

Caveau, Bar du, 176

Cazes, Marcellin, 14

Chambon, Paul, 15

Charbon, Café, 134–135

Charette, La, 16, 86

Chevalier, Maurice, 70–71

Chez Gladines, 138

Chope des Puces, La, 157–158

Cirque d'Hiver, Le, 15, 71–73

Clichy, Place de, 44, 82, 86

Coupole, La, **22–24**, 38, 53

Crane, Hart, 50–51